W9-BON-531

Seriously God?

SPIRITUAL INSIGHTS WHEN LIFE
SUDDENLY CHANGES

Volume 1

CRYSTAL MCDOWELL

© 2016 Crystal McDowell

All rights reserved. No portion of this book may be reproduced, stored in a retrieval system, or transmitted in any form or by any means-electronic, mechanical, photocopy, recording, scanning, or other-except for brief quotations in critical reviews or articles, without prior written permission of the publisher.

Unless otherwise indicated, all Scripture quotations are from the ESVR Bible (The Holy Bible, English Standard VersionR), copyright c 2001 by Crossway, a publishing ministry of Good News Publishers. Used by permission. All rights reserved.

Dedicated to the 5 Brightest Stars in my life:
Jonathan, Jasmine, Jaida, Janelle, and Jessica.
Truly beautiful gifts from God.

Children are a heritage from the LORD.
Psalm 127:3

Crystal McDowell

CONTENTS

Crystal McDowell

Acknowledgements

There's never a time greater for the light of true friendship to shine than when life gets tough. I'm grateful to God, my heavenly Father, who led family and friends to support me through my difficult days. Special love to my parents, Christopher and Sue Duncan as well as Dr. Matthew and Hortense McDowell—your support and prayers are felt and appreciated. My supportive and faithful siblings: Jamie, Kristen, Christopher (Vonda), and Daniel (Tiffany)—I couldn't have made it without your encouraging phone calls and acts of kindness. To my five beautiful children who put up with many 'OYO' dinner nights throughout the years when I had deadlines to meet—I love each of you to the moon and back. I also want to give a shout out to my mentor, Judy Hanks, for her unwavering words of strength and listening ears, as I searched my way through the dark days. To my first love, I will always love and pray for you.

This journey wouldn't have been possible without the gift of friendship from many people. Sean and Dana, Tracy, Karen, Diane, Jamillah—you stayed on me and with me through so much—my heart is full of appreciation. My Bible study ladies: Margaret, Mernala, Megan, Stephanie, Jackie, Margie, Ann, Laurie, Laura, Nayoka, Michelle, Leesa, Georgia, Wendy, Kate, Lisa, Ashley, and Tessa—so much laughter and tears in the presence of the Lord—you all are my joy!

Special thanks and love to my brothers and sisters in Christ at Eastview Christian Church for your unconditional love and support: Mike and Sarah, Jim, Kim H., Rosie, Lisa, Larry and Kelly, Kim B., Kim M., Clayt, Bob, Gail, Clete, and Wilma.

To my girlfriends who lovingly read and reread my book for me: Judy, Jackie, Tara, Michelle, Jamillah, Diane, Allison, and Karen…love, love, and more love to you.

To Josh Wiley and Corey Alderin for their faith and support through Telling Ministries—without whom daughtersofthecreator.com would have never been possible—you guys rock!

There's many more people than I have room to mention; however, there's a list of names in heaven in which God will rain down blessings on those who gave, supported, prayed, and loved my family through thick and thin. God bless you!

The greatest praise and adoration remains for my Lord and Savior Jesus Christ for His unwavering love, grace, mercy, and guidance that gave me the strength to press my way through adversity towards His marvelous plan for my life.

Introduction

Years ago after struggling with God's peace over a major decision, I saw myself walking a tightrope and way below was a net. The Holy Spirit assured me that if I was knocked off the tightrope of life—He would catch me. Fast forward twenty plus years later, I hit the net…hard.

When my life suddenly changed, I asked "Seriously God?" almost every day. Even though I wasn't perfect, I faithfully followed my calling: a committed wife and stay-at-home mother of five children, a Christian freelance writer/editor/speaker, a servant in church ministry, and a Bible teacher.

My life fell apart even though I was praying, fasting, seeking godly counsel, and holding on to what I knew was right. The pace of sudden change wouldn't slow down enough for me. I desperately sought answers from God to make sense of the chaos. Somehow by the grace of God, I kept moving forward.

I drew strength reading about real people with problems in the Bible. God didn't skip over their sins any more than their triumphs. Elijah was one of those people, who were sometimes brave, fearful, powerful, and weak. He demonstrated great faith by calling down fire from heaven and later, he would demonstrate great fear by running away from Jezebel. He was real.

We know Elijah was like us because of James 5:17 "Elijah was a man with a nature like ours." As believers we will have times of extraordinary faith and courage along with times of desperate trembling and anxiety. We have a real God who helps us with our real problems in this lifetime.

Each section break draws from Elijah's experience and how we can glean hope when we are knocked off the tightrope of life. This devotional book is meant to be a companion for those who are struggling with change in their lives. It's about getting caught in the net with God, when everything else seemingly falls apart. It's distinctly for those who've realized that God is the only way to get through the tough places, even as we ask the honest question: *Seriously God?*

Section 1: God's got It

"You shall drink from the brook, and I have commanded the ravens to feed you there."

1 Kings 17:4

Background Scripture: 1 Kings 17:1-7

Section 1: God's got It

And we know that for those who love God all things
work together for good.
Romans 8:28

When the Israelites turned against God towards idolatry, Elijah prayed earnestly that it would not rain for three years. (Leviticus 26:18) The drought over the nation was a serious hardship for the people who depended on the crops for survival. Everybody suffered, even those followed God and didn't bow the knee to Baal. Some may have died or watched loved ones starve to death because of the judgment.

It may have been difficult for them to believe in the midst of their suffering that God was in control. No Christian alive is untouched by sin, either ours or someone else's. Just as the sun shines on the just and the unjust (Matthew 5:45), tragedy affects everyone regardless of their faith or lack thereof.

Saying "God's got it" and living like "God's got it" are two different ballgames altogether. Most of us know that God is in control. We know that we couldn't wake up and start our day without God. We recognize His hand over our lives and the lives of our families. Yet, when calamity, disappointment, or despair finds its way into our lives we wonder, "Does God got this?"

My drought experience was losing my marriage, home, and everything that I believed was secure about my life. It wasn't a slow chipping away; rather it was like a tornado swooped in and scattered my life. There were many times when I wondered if God really had it under control. I felt like a pinball rolling all over the place, because this wasn't the way it was supposed to happen. I had to surrender my futile attempts to control the situation. For some reason, I still thought I could figure a way out. I finally gave up and prayed "I got nothing Lord."

It doesn't matter the nature of our drought experience as much as knowing who is in control. Once we grasp the concept that God is in control, we can have peace in the midst of our personal drought. During the famine, the Lord hid Elijah by the Brook Cherith and provided him food brought by ravens. Elijah stayed there until the brook dried up. Because God had a purpose for Elijah to fulfill, He would make a way to keep him alive.

God will also make a way for us to survive, just like He did for Elijah. He may not show us how everything is going to work out in the end, but He will fill our hearts with hope and give us strength to press forward.

I didn't get all my questions answered from God, but I did receive His presence when I was the loneliest, His power when I was the weakest, His wisdom when I couldn't tell right from wrong nor up from down, His peace when my mind and soul were wracked with pain, and His love when I felt utterly rejected. The twenty-five devotionals in this section focus on trusting that God has everything in control.

Day 1: Seriously God?

> While he was still speaking.
> Job 1:16

When Job was hit with disaster after disaster, the scriptures began with "while he was still speaking". Before one servant could finish explaining the sudden loss of Job's property, another was out of breath trying to explain another loss—and before he could finish—another servant began with the news of his children's death. Although Job didn't accuse God of any wrongdoing, he reeled from the pain and sought to make sense of it.

Sometimes when we are going through great pain and loss one after the other, we may want to throw up our hands and ask "Seriously God?" We live in a culture that believes if we do everything the right way, then our lives will be comfortable and carefree.

However, this isn't the truth of scripture. Rather, Jesus said that "in this world you will have trouble" (John 16:33), and Paul wrote to Timothy that "everyone who wants to live a godly life in Christ Jesus will be persecuted" (2 Timothy 3:12). As believers of Christ Jesus, we must come to embrace that suffering will be a part of our journey, whether we choose it or not.

Looking from the outside, many people may wonder why we became Christians and hold to our testimony in spite of suffering and persecution. It's because as believers, we have the hope of God in our hearts through the indwelling presence of the Holy Spirit. We press on not because we hope to do well in this temporary life, we press on towards the future hope of heaven.

Let's not give up when the going gets tough. Instead, let's recommit our spirits and transform our thinking towards God's strength and presence to help us carry on. We were created for a purpose, and He has a great plan for those who press on in spite of the trials.

Prayer:

Dear Lord, I don't understand why all this is happening to me. However I'm encouraged to trust in You anyway. Strengthen my faith in You. Amen.

Faith Action:

Write a note to God about your questions, seal it, and write today's date on it. Reopen it after you've completed this book and see how God has been faithful to you.

Day 2: Looking to God

We do not know what to do, but our eyes are on you.
2 Chronicles 20:12

King Jehoshaphat found himself in a difficult place. A great multitude of other nations were preparing to attack Judah. There was no great plan of defense against their enemies. Their backs were against the wall and time was short. In response to this threat, Jehoshaphat humbled himself to seek the Lord, proclaimed a national fast, and prayed publicly for deliverance.

His prayer reminded God of who He was "O LORD, God of our fathers, are you not God in heaven? You rule over all the kingdoms of the nations. In your hand are power and might, so that none is able to withstand you." (2 Chronicles 20:6) In the assembly of the people, including babies and small children, Jehoshaphat cried out for God's hand to save them from their enemies. He admitted their powerlessness and inability to fight. Their eyes were on God.

The Lord delivered them in a miraculous way, their enemies completely destroyed each other and left Judah all the spoils of war. Can this happen for us today? Can we call out to God for deliverance, praying like Jehoshaphat and looking to God?

Absolutely! God is the same today, yesterday, and forevermore. He is no respecter of persons, there is no favoritism with Him. He will deliver us from our enemy, Satan.

The questions are: are we willing to do what it takes? Are we willing to fast at times? Are we willing to look to God first, before looking to people to help us along the way? Are we willing to publicly confess our allegiance to God and His ability to save?

Prayer:

Dear Lord, without You I can do nothing. I look to You to deliver and steer me on the right course of life. You are my strength to overcome the enemies in my life. Amen.

Faith Action:

If possible, look up to the sky, speak to God about what He has done for you in the past, and let Him know that you are looking to Him for deliverance.

Day 3: Who's the Boss?

The king's heart is a stream of water in the hand of the
LORD; he turns it wherever he will.
Proverbs 21:1

In the mid-1980's, there was a popular TV sitcom
called "Who's the Boss?" This show highlighted a
single mom with a great career, and her need for an
unconventional housekeeper. It highlighted how many
of us think we are the "boss." However, the influence
of our family, friends, coworkers, life circumstances,
and earthly bosses seem to boss us around.

Those who live according to the dictates of this world
will focus their attentions around pleasing their boss in
order to move up in the workplace. However, this can
often lead to disappointment, because people will
always let them down in one way or another. A
people-pleasing attitude in life will eventually lead to a
mighty crash of dreams and life purpose.

As believers, we are compelled to keep our focus on
God and not man. Jesus is the Boss of us, and we must
continually seek His wisdom and direction for our
vocational choices and promotions. Paul admonished
in Colossians 3:23-25 "Whatever you do, work at it
with all your heart, as working for the Lord, not for
human masters, since you know that you will receive

an inheritance from the Lord as a reward. It is the Lord Christ you are serving."

If we look to our earthly bosses to give us the accolades, rewards, or promotions that we feel we deserve, we will fall short and become disillusioned in our work. God is the Boss of our bosses even if they don't know it. He will control every decision that affects our work and use it for His glory. As we look to God as our heavenly Boss and trust in Him to give us wisdom, insight, and the strength to do our job well, we will exceed human expectations and pave the way for future rewards.

Prayer:

Dear Lord, I confess the times that I've focused on myself and other people more than focusing on You. Lead my thoughts to trust in You more. Amen.

Faith Action:

Pray for those who have authority over you. Ask the Lord to give you favor in their eyes as you glorify Him.

Day 4: I Am

God said to Moses, "I AM WHO I AM."
Exodus 3:14

When God called Moses to lead His people from
Egypt, Moses asked, "What is his name? What shall I
say to them?" God's response set Him apart from the
Egyptian pagan gods because He fully encompassed
everything. "I Am" was enough for the Israelites, and
He is enough for us today.

There are times when we forget that He is the great "I
Am" of our lives because we get distracted by
busyness, families, careers, etc. However, sometimes
we need to step back and reflect on God as—I Am. He
is greater than all of our concerns and able to take care
of everything we have before Him.

When we are sick, He is the Healer. When we are lost,
He is the Way. When we are in danger, He is the
Protector. When we are in need, He is the Provider.
When we are under attack, He is the Defender. When
we are scared, He is the Comforter. When we are
lonely, He is Emmanuel (God with us). When we were
dead in our sins, He is the Giver of life.

If we really want to know the great "I Am", we can
begin our prayers with everything that we know God

is now, was in the past, and will be in the future. As we pray with the mindset of knowing the "I Am" at the beginning of our prayers, we will find our faith emboldened to pray according to His will, and not according to our circumstances.

As believers of Jesus Christ, we have "I Am" on our side, who is willing to be all things for us and through us. We can live in confidence that the God within us is greater than anything we need.

Prayer:

Dear Lord, forgive me for the times that I've forgotten that You are "I Am" and everything I need in this life. Restore my faith according to your word. Amen.

Faith Action:

Find a name of God that will encourage your faith to overcome a difficult situation. Pray to Him by His name and believe in His ability to do above and beyond what you ask.

Day 5: For Your Good

For those who are called according to his purpose.
Romans 8:28

When a major life crisis hit me a years ago, I remember sitting before God and wondering how anything good could come out it. As I struggled day by day, I came back to God with this question "What happened to my life?"

As a mature believer, I'm acquainted with Romans 8:28, as many people have reminded me that God is able to make my tough situation work for my good. However, in the moment, I didn't take immediate comfort from it. I was in the trenches of my life, and it was difficult to see anything beyond that.

Yet, I kept pressing into the Lord. At times it was rough, I would plead my case like Job did—haven't I done the right things? I would express my disappointment with many tears and pleading before God at night. However, every morning I would wake up to the refreshing and encouraging presence of God that gave me strength to press forward with the day.

God is faithful to all of us. He allows a situation to make us more tough and tender as believers. We become tougher in our faith by trusting in God despite difficulties. We also become tender in our response to others as we've known how hard and lonely life can get sometimes. All of the events of our past will turn for our good, although we still have many unresolved remnants of painful experiences.

God is good all the time. He uses our hard times to make us more like His Son, Jesus Christ. We are strengthened by this hope and His promise to turn our tough times for our good, regardless of what the situation looks like.

Prayer:

Dear Lord, I pray that You would increase my faith when times are tough. I want to press forward in faith rather than stumble in fear. Help me to trust You more. Amen.

Faith Action:

Think of a situation in your past that God used to turn for your good. Use that memory to encourage yourself in your present situation.

Day 6: Come-to-Jesus Moment

God is not man, that he should lie, or a son of man,
that he should change his mind.
Numbers 23:19

Have you ever had a come-to-Jesus moment? Usually, this is an intervention with someone when you need them to deal with a truth. But, have you ever had a "come to Jesus moment" with Jesus?

Recently, I was bombarded with problems that had no answers. I'd go to sleep and wake up trying to figure them out. I finally became tired of being on the crazy train and decided it was a come-to-Jesus moment. I sat at my window, looked towards the sky, and asked Jesus to give me clarity on recent decisions.

When we come to this place in our relationship with Jesus, our decisions aren't made carelessly, we pray and seek God's direction and wisdom. Sometimes we struggle to keep up and wonder if we made the right decisions. We may need to hold up our Bible and humbly state that we are following His word to the best of our abilities. We also can confess our sins and shortcomings, if they are a reason in the hold up of our answers to the pressing problems.

Finally, in our come-to-Jesus moment, we surrender our will to the Lord's will. With this last confession, we will experience peace that will bypass our hearts and minds. We will feel better, because we know that God has heard our request and He will work it out according to His will.

Knowing that God won't ever lie nor take back something in the Bible, gives us the confidence to move forward in faith. We can take God at His word every single time. He will never ever fail us.

Prayer:

Dear Lord, You are my confidence in making decisions and seeking your wisdom on what to do. I know that your word is genuine and true, so build my faith to trust You more. Amen.

Faith Action:

Write down and memorize 1 John 5:14-15. Pray it out loud every time you feel doubtful about God answering your prayers.

Day 7: God Knows

Go, call your husband, and come here.
John 4:16

The Samaritan woman was minding her own business when she had an encounter with Jesus. He asked her for water and she questioned Him because Jews didn't converse Samaritans. Jesus spoke to her about the living water in which she would never thirst again. She asked for this water, and Jesus told her to get her husband. She replied, "I have no husband." Jesus replied that she answered correctly, because of her five previous husbands, and the one who was with her wasn't her husband.

The Samaritan woman was not the only woman in that day struggling with her relationships; however, she was the one Jesus chose to reveal Himself to in that city. She may have been an outcast because of her choices, but Jesus knew and made a way for her to know Him.

Jesus knew about her before she was at the well, because nothing is hidden from His sight. He still asked her the question about her husband, because she needed to speak the truth. Just like her, our hidden sins aren't hidden from God. He sees everything and longs for us to come clean to ourselves and to Him.

19

God knows, and He doesn't give up on those He loves. God knows, and He will do whatever it takes to bring us back to the place where we belong. God knows, and just as Jesus dealt with the Samaritan woman—He's not looking for an opportunity to beat our heads down in shame. He wants us to come to the place of repentance and trust in Him for strength to overcome our weaknesses.

The woman's testimony brought many Samaritans to know Jesus. Just like the Samaritan woman, we can be healed, set free, and used by God to draw many to Jesus when we are willing to speak the truth to Him.

Prayer:

Dear Lord, You know me. You know my heart longs to know and please You. Give me the strength to walk in truth for my life. Amen.

Faith Action:

Is there something that God knows about you that needs to be confessed? Read 1 John 1:9, confess your sins, and receive forgiveness.

Day 8: Did God Say?

Did God actually say, 'You shall not eat of any tree in
the garden'?
Genesis 3:1

Adam and Eve were created perfect by God. Before
one conversation with Satan, their life with each other
was blissful and peaceful. In addition, they enjoyed a
close relationship with their Creator who would visit
with them regularly in the cool of the day. Yet, one
question would completely change the earth forever.
Satan questioned what God made clear to Adam: every
tree was free for them to eat, except the tree of the
knowledge of good and evil.

Satan is still tempting us with questions about God. Is
God real? Are you saved? Do you need to wait for a
spouse? Or do you need to stay with your spouse? Do
you need to give tithes and offerings? Do you need to
pray every day? Do you need to know the Bible?

These questions from the devil are meant to cast doubt
on God, so that we can be deceived, just as Eve was.
Jesus demonstrated for us what we are to do when
Satan questions the motives and intentions of God. In
His interaction with the devil, Jesus quoted the
accurate word of God. He didn't entertain Satan with

conversation like Eve did, He simply said the word, and that was it.

We need to answer Satan's questions in the same manner. God is real because of Psalms 19:1. We are saved because of Ephesians 2:8. We wait for a husband because of Psalm 37:4. We remain married because of Hebrews 13:4. We give our finances because of Malachi 3:10. We pray every day because of 1 Thessalonians 5:17. We know the Bible because of John 8:32.

We have the answers to Satan's questions nestled in the word of God. Be like Jesus...speak the word and move forward to do your Father's business.

Prayer:

Dear Lord, help me to become more discerning when the devil tempts me towards unbelief. I need your word to be a light to my path. Amen.

Faith Action:

Is Satan tempting you with questions to doubt God's love and mercy? Meditate on 2 Corinthians 2:10-11, Ephesians 6:10-20, and James 4:7-8. Find a scriptures that speaks directly to your heart to stand against the tempting of Satan.

Day 9: Does God hear Me?

He hears the prayer of the righteous.
Proverbs 15:29

Have you ever felt abandoned by God? You've prayed over and over again—and yet it doesn't seem like anything is happening. You've called out to God to intervene, and at times, it seems like things have gotten worse. You keep reading your Bible and living righteously; however, life still seems to have taken a direction that you hadn't planned on.

Sometimes it's difficult to believe that God longs to hear and answer our prayers. Yet He does. No matter who loves us right now, their love pales in comparison to the overwhelming and steadfast love of God.

We forget the mighty spiritual battle in the heavenly places that happens when we pray. Because of our prayers, Satan will do everything he can to tempt us towards avoiding a consistent prayer life. He doesn't mind us being busy with church work or with our families as long as we don't pray. He knows that our prayers bring the result of God's will regardless of the resistance.

God hears the prayers of His children and answers according to His will. He wants us to continue

23

pressing forward in prayer regardless of the time of day or our situations in life. Just because we don't "feel" like God hears our prayers, doesn't mean that He's not answering them. When we humble ourselves to pray and confess our sins, the Lord opens doors that we didn't even know existed.

There is great joy when we see the evidence of God answering our prayers. We wait and pray expectantly against great mountain tops of discouragement, despair, and unmet longings. He is more than able to answer in His perfect timing. God hears and answers our prayers because He is a faithful and loving Father.

Prayer:

Dear Lord, I look to You to answer my prayers. I seek your wisdom and direction from the Holy Spirit on how to pray every day. Help me to continue to pray. Amen.

Faith Action:

Has your prayer life been inconsistent? Try starting with a five minute prayer in the morning and at night. Continue to build your prayer time with God.

Day 10: Be Still

Be still, and know that I am God.
Psalm 46:10

Have you ever watched a child squirm in church? Their parents often turn to them and say, "Be still!" Give them a few minutes and they are squirming again. It's what we come to expect of children, especially when they are too young to understand the service.

But what if God is telling us to "Be still!"? How hard is that? Many of us will now sympathize with the squirming child. When we are surrounded by difficulty and tempted to make things happen in our own way, being still is the last thing we want to hear. We want to move, and we want God to move according to our prayers.

However, just like the child, it may be beyond our understanding, and we must be still in trusting that God knows what He is doing, even when we don't. Being still is more than just not doing anything at all. Being still may mean that we need to take more time to pray, read the Bible, or fast for a few days. Being still may mean that we need to calm our anxious hearts and know that God is taking care of us. Being still may mean that we need to take some time alone in solitude and retreat from the busyness of our lives.

Whatever being still may mean to us individually, the concept of being still in the Lord encompasses knowing that God is in control. The fact that He is God should be enough for us. We are blessed to know that He is our God who cares for us and will never forsake us when times get tough. Be still, and know that our God will take care of us.

Prayer:

Dear Lord, help me be still and trust in You more. Calm my anxious heart and mind so that I can know You better through my situation. Amen.

Faith Action:

Are you feeling anxious in your heart and unable to be still in His presence? Find a quiet and calm place to read Psalm 23. Go slowly over each verse and ask the Lord to calm your inner being.

Day 11: God Can

Is anything too hard for the LORD?
Genesis 18:14

There are many times in our Christian journey where we will be tested in our faith. We know that God can do the impossible, but will He do it for us? It's difficult when we are hit by the hard stuff of life, especially when it's our family members or friends in trouble. We want to believe God can; however, we are tempted to let our minds wander to the worst possible scenarios.

It's in those days that we must focus on God's word and His ways (i.e. following the way of love, peace, forgiveness). As we turn to the truth of scriptures, we are encouraged to keep our faith because we know that He works everything for our good. We know that He hears our prayers and answers them according to His will. We know that the gates of hell can't prevail against the church. We know that God is in the midst, when two or three of us are gathered in His name.

When we focus on God's ways, we remember how He kept His promise to Abraham even though it was humanly impossible for an elderly couple to have a baby. We remember how He intervened for the children of Israel by freeing them from slavery and

27

leading them to the Promised Land. We remember how God, through the power of the Holy Spirit, gave David the courage and strength to defeat Goliath. We also remember that God's character never changes, and what He did for those in the Bible, He can still do today. (Genesis 18:1-21, Joshua 21:43-45, 1 Samuel 17)

We meditate on the many different ways that God answered our prayers when we are absolutely without hope nor strength. We meditate on how He healed our bodies, restored our marriages, saved our prodigals, and blessed our homes. God can do it. God will do it in His own timing and plan.

Prayer:

Dear Lord, help me to build my faith through the reading of your word and the remembering of your faithfulness in my past. Amen.

Faith Action:

Do you think your situation is too hard for God? If so, step outside to take in the creation that God made out of nothing. Allow the Holy Spirit to comfort your heart with faith.

Day 15: I Believe But...

I believe; help my unbelief!
Mark 9:24

I can't imagine the unbearable pain of the father in Mark 9:14-29 where his son had been controlled by a demon since his childhood. This child would writhe uncontrollably, grind his teeth, foam at the mouth, and seemed like he was dead at times. If that wasn't enough, the demon would lead the boy to fire and water in efforts to take his life. The father must have been very frustrated, tired, and discouraged.

He originally brought his son to the disciples who couldn't help him and were arguing with the scribes. When Jesus showed up, the father shared "But if you can do anything, have compassion on us and help us". Jesus responded, "If you can! All things are possible for one who believes". The father helplessly replied, "I believe; help my unbelief!" Jesus cast the demon out and the boy was made whole.

As believers, we know that God can heal and make whole. We know that God cares about the impossible situations in our lives. Yet even still, we struggle with our unbelief because we are looking squarely at the impossibility of our situation.

Yet, the more impossible the situation, the more glory God receives. We can pray in that moment "help my unbelief!" It's our Father in heaven who loves and allows us to share our hearts without shame. The Lord always responds to the faith of His children, regardless of our unbelief. We refuse to narrowly focus on the impossibility, and instead refocus on God's love and greatness over our lives.

God understands our struggles with unbelief. As we continue to walk in prayer and strong Biblical knowledge, our faith will overcome unbelief.

Prayer:

Dear Lord, help my unbelief in this situation. Strengthen my faith through your word and comfort me in times of prayer. I trust You, even when I don't understand everything around me. Amen.

Faith Action:

Do you ever feel like "I believe, but…"? If so, you aren't alone. Read and pray over Mark 9:22-29. Meditate on truth of Mark 9:23.

Day 16: Jehovah Jireh

The LORD will provide.
Genesis 22:14

Years ago, I was completely lost on how I was going to provide for my family. I fell on my knees before God and pleaded for wisdom on how to move forward. I felt the Holy Spirit speak to my heart, "when you need it, it will be there."

Fast forward to the present time, God has proven His faithfulness to provide every step of the way. There were many times I had no idea how a situation was going to work out, and God always provided. Abraham also had a faith dilemma, he obeyed God's command to take his beloved son and sacrifice him in the land of Moriah. He had no idea how it was going to work out, yet when Isaac asked about the sacrifice, his response was "God will provide…"

Many times we want God to show us how He's going to provide before we take the actual steps of obedience. Not with Abraham, he immediately stepped out in faith. It's in our steps of obedience that we most clearly stake out our faith in His ability to provide for us. If we had everything that we wanted, why would we need to ask God for it? It's our faith in the invisible, but real God that projects us to believing in the impossible.

The Lord promises to provide all of our needs according to His riches in glory. (Philippians 4:19) It's our responsibility to request and trust in God's perfect timing for our needs. We won't necessarily get everything we want; however, He will provide for those things that we need for survival, peace, and hope in Him.

Prayer:

Dear Lord, I look to You to provide everything I need to survive in this world. Help me to continue to walk in obedience as I trust in You with all of my heart. Amen.

Faith Action:

What are you asking God to provide? Pray to Jehovah Jireh to provide everything you need in His perfect timing.

Day 17: Stay True

Let us draw near with a true heart.
Hebrews 10:22

As believers in the Lord Jesus Christ, we know it's wrong to tell a lie—but we must be careful to not live a lie. We live a lie when our lives don't match up to what God's word teaches us. Sometimes we find ourselves making excuses for ourselves, and living a lie. If we don't pay close attention, we may not even be aware of it.

If our hearts aren't true to God, it will affect our assurance in the faith and our confidence in God will be weakened. We may find that our prayer life has become difficult. We may lose the desire to be involved in our churches. We could find ourselves pulled closer to the world and less towards God.

We can stay on the true path of life if we stay in God's word every single day. Reading, meditating, memorizing, and praying the scriptures will always reveal truth in our lives. We can grow in the faith and live our lives in freedom, if we know the truth of God's word.

When we are true to God, we can be true to ourselves and those who are around us. We don't have to be afraid of falling, because we are standing firm in the faith and walking in truth. Truth will be evident in our walk, and God will use us to help others stay true as well.

Jesus said that He is the way, the truth, and the life. (John 14:6) When we walk in truth, we are most like Jesus. Staying true to our God, faith, and loved ones gives us courage to step out and believe the Lord to accomplish the great things.

Prayer:

Dear Lord, help me to stay true to Jesus and the teachings of the Bible. I need You to always lead me into all truth every day. Amen.

Faith Action:

Do you struggle with being true to God? If so, take time today to confess your weakness and begin to overcome with truth with God's word.

Day 18: Steady Yourself

Do not be anxious about anything.
Philippians 4:6

Have you ever found yourself worrying about the future? Some of us worry if we will ever be married, and some of us worry about staying married. We can worry about our jobs, children, safety, security, etc. Some people say that 80% of what we worry about will never happen. This is good, but what about the 20% that does happen? More things to worry about...

When we find ourselves stumbling down the worry valley, we can pull out of it rather quickly if we learn how to steady ourselves. This steadiness isn't built on some self-help method of repeating the same things over and over, while hoping that it will sink in one day. Our complete and solid foundation of resisting worry is steadfastly rooted in our knowledge of God's word

First, we think about who God was in the Bible and recognize how He showed Himself faithful from Genesis to Revelation. Afterwards, we meditate on what He has done to show Himself faithful to us in our present day lives and situations. Lastly, we think about His promise to one day take us to heaven to live eternally in joy and peace.

After we steadied ourselves about who God was, is, and will be, we began to thank Him for His many blessings over our lives. Our time of thankfulness is followed by our request or petition that we need from Him. Our request is made in the light of God's faithfulness which we know to be true. We lay our desires at the foot of the cross and turn our thoughts towards everything that is true, honorable, just, pure, lovely, commendable, excellent, and praiseworthy.

This regular practice takes a little time at first; however, the discipline of it will strengthen our resolve to steady ourselves. The Lord will guard our heart and mind so that we will be filled with peace that we don't even understand.

Prayer:

Dear Lord, I pray that I will learn to steady myself on the knowledge and goodness of your faithfulness. I turn away from worrying and turn to You in faith. Amen.

Faith Action:

Memorize and practice Philippians 4:6-8 whenever you are tempted to worry.

Day 19: Tearing Down Mental Strongholds

Take every thought captive to obey Christ.
2 Corinthians 10:5

Have you ever struggled with recurring thoughts that weren't edifying? It could be a memory from a hurtful conversation, or it could be replaying a scene in your life that was sinful. As much as you would prefer to *not* think this way, it feels impossible to control your thoughts, and you are constantly being brought down because of them.

While this is a common struggle for believers, we don't have to live under mental strongholds that constantly bring us down. Our Father in heaven longs for us to experience mental freedom. He wants us to have the mind of Christ, so that we can freely do His will without restraints. Yet mental strongholds don't go down because we want them to, we must actively and intently bring them down.

Our thoughts can be managed if we are willing to train our minds to think differently through the word of God. The first step to being free from mental strongholds is to pray for God's help and direction. We confess any sins on our part that may be feeding the strongholds. It's also helpful to ask God to help us stay on guard especially when we are less ready to deal with the strongholds (i.e. feeling overtired, stressed, overworked).

We can find a scripture that speaks to our hearts and minds concerning our situation such as Philippians 4:7-8 and 1 Peter 1:13. If we struggle with fear, we speak 2 Timothy 1:7, if we struggle with feeling alone, we speak Hebrews 13:5, or if we struggle with doubt, we speak Hebrews 11:6. Mental strongholds are defenseless against God's word mixed with our faith.

Prayer:

Dear Lord, I pray for the strength and resiliency to resist destructive mental strongholds. Help me to meditate and speak your word for deliverance. Amen.

Faith Action:

Look up one of the scriptures in the passage above and use it as a prayer for deliverance over mental strongholds.

Day 20: What-ifs

My days are past; my plans are broken off.
Job 17:11

Has your mind ever been besieged by the 'what-ifs'? What if my marriage doesn't work out? What if I never get married or have children? What if the stock market plunges? What if my company lays me off? What if I don't pass this test? What if my child gets addicted to drugs or alcohol? What if someone hacks into my bank account and steals all of my money?

It's not the absence of 'what-ifs' that will give us peace, but rather our choice to not let the 'what-ifs' rule our lives. We know that there is always some kind of risk in this life. We live in a sinful world that is only going to get worse every day until Jesus returns.

We can find our peace when we settle in our spirits that God is in control. Knowing this gives us hope to keep moving forward, even when our plans go awry. God's plan lives will always trump our plans. He will engineer everything to work towards our good, even when we are blinded by the troubles before us.

There is hope for those who have put their trust in Jesus. He doesn't want us anxious about every possible turn of life. We can overcome our anxious thoughts by praying to God and relaxing in His peace. (Philippians 4:6-8) We can also discipline our minds to focus on being thankful about everything that has gone right, instead of focusing on all the things that could possibly go wrong.

Our peace is tied into our faith in an all-powerful, all-knowing, and always present God. We aren't left to the mercy of 'what-ifs'; rather we are carefully protected and guided by the Lord of the universe.

Prayer:

Dear Lord, I want to let go of all the 'what-ifs' in my life. Restore right thinking so that I can trust in You with all of my heart. Amen.

Faith Action:

For every doubting 'what-if' in your life, write out a word from the Bible that demonstrates faith in God.

Day 21: Why Me?

In all this Job did not sin or charge God with wrong.
Job 1:22

Have you ever gone through a long trial that has stretched you spiritually, emotionally, and physically? And all the while you're asking the question: why me?

What makes us think that we shouldn't have times of suffering just like our brothers and sisters across the world? Should we not have times of crying, sleepless nights, and overwhelming disappointments? Should we expect everything to always go as we plan? No, not if we want to grow in our faith.

If we ask the question 'why me' in trials and temptations, should we then also ask the same question in times of blessings? We don't usually hear anyone ask God 'why me?' when things are going well. Why should we have a relationship with Jesus Christ instead of living in darkness? Why should we expect to have joy and peace in the midst of a storm? Why should we enjoy the grace of God that gives us strength to make it day to day?

Why me? Because we are uniquely chosen by God to go through this time of trial to become everything He wants us to be.

Why me? Because no pain nor tears are ever wasted in the kingdom of God.

Why me? Because He is preparing us for a greater glory, in order to draw more people to the cross.

Why me? Because we're growing into this relationship with God slowly, but assured of His presence and hand over our lives.

Prayer:

Dear Lord, help me to resist the pity party for myself and trust that You have everything I need to make it day to day. Strengthen my faith in You. Amen.

Faith Action:

Every time you hear "why me?" in your heart, ask the question "why not me?" and pray to God to help you learn whatever He needs for you in this time of trial.

Day 22: Did I Miss Something?

Why did you ever send me?
Exodus 5:22

Moses was minding his own business when God showed up with a burning bush. When God told Moses that He was sending him to set the Israelites free, Moses resisted. Yet, God worked around Moses' inhibitions by using his brother, Aaron, as a spokesperson. The brothers went first to the Israelites, and then to Pharaoh seeking the release of God's people.

The same day of the request, Pharaoh refused to let the people go and made the Israelites worked more heavily than before Moses showed up. As a result of their suffering, they refused to listen to Moses. After all the hesitation Moses had before God, after he went to the Israelites, and after he went to Pharaoh, Moses found himself on the outs with both the Egyptians and the Israelites. He was supposed to lead the people out of Egypt, but it didn't seem to be going in that direction.

Have you ever been there? We follow everything we believe that God wants us to do, and the result seems worse than if we had never started. Yet, what we call a delay, God uses as a part of His plan to get us where we need to be.

For example, by being tasked more heavily, the people were more ready to leave Egypt. By digging his heels against God, Pharaoh's stubbornness ushered in the great plagues that became a powerful expression of God's power and glory. By being tested and doubted by the people, Moses developed thick skin in preparation of leading a discontented and stubborn people to the Promised Land.

If we find our spiritual calling and journey becoming more difficult, it doesn't necessarily mean that we missed something. It could mean that God has testing, endurance, perseverance, and long-suffering to get us where He wants us to be for His purpose and calling.

Prayer:

Dear Lord, I need your intervention to give me discernment so that I don't miss it. Help me to persevere when my calling gets difficult and I don't understand everything that is going on. Amen.

Faith Action:

Do you feel that you've missed something along the way? Take the time to reflect and pray for God's guidance.

Day 23: Mary Stayed

The disciples went back to their homes…
but Mary stood weeping.
John 20:10-11

Jesus was mercilessly crucified in front of his followers who knew Him to be innocent and righteous. Three days later, the disciples found out through Mary Magdalene and other women that Jesus' body was missing. Peter and John ran to the tomb, looked around in bewilderment, and went home. But not Mary…she stayed there. As a result, our Lord appeared to Mary first and comforted her. She went back and boldly announced to the disciples that Jesus was alive.

What do you do in times of bewilderment? The world turns to many things, such as alcohol, drugs, recreation, and the arms of another in order to find something to numb the pain. Yet as believers, we are to stay firm in the faith and wait on the Lord to show us next steps. Just as Mary stayed and wept, we too, may find ourselves weeping before the Lord in the early morning or late hours of the night.

Yet if we stay, He will meet us there. The Lord will give us comfort and hope through the Holy Spirit and His word. When we wait patiently on God, He will not disappoint nor abandon those who serve Him out of a pure heart. We stay when everyone else runs away back home. We stay on our knees and call out to our Father. We stay in the word of God for our strength and peace in the midst of craziness. We stay active in our church fellowship and service to the body of Christ.

Our faithfulness, one moment at a time, isn't lost on the Lord. He knows where we are and what we need from Him. Just stay and wait.

Prayer:

Dear Lord, I've been grieved in my spirit and I make myself stay at your feet. Show yourself to me so that I may be comforted and strengthened to move forward. Amen.

Faith Action:

Next time you are hit with a problem—stay and wait on Jesus in prayer.

Day 24: Tussling with God

And Jacob was left alone. And a man wrestled with
him until the breaking of the day.
Genesis 32:24

Have you felt like you were tussling with God? You
prayed and believed for your healing, but it hasn't
happened yet. You believe that He has a greater plan
for your life, but nothing is looking good on the
horizon. You get frustrated because you witness the
prosperity of wicked people, while you languish with
unpaid bills and less income.

We can wrestle with God like Jacob did. Jacob went
back and forth until the Lord touched his hip socket.
While it might've ended Jacob's wrestling match, it
didn't immediately end their interaction. Jacob
wouldn't let go of the Lord, even though he was told it
was time to do so. He refused to let go until the Lord
blessed him.

Wrestling is a sport of close contact and we will know
our opponent better than we know most people. When
we wrestle with God, we will know Him better. Do we
hold on until He blesses us? Or do we let go too early
without considering that God has a purpose for us
even in the wrestling?

We know that our blessings can come through the Lord, if we don't let go too soon. The Lord could've shaken off Jacob whenever He wanted. However, Jacob had to reach out in faith and hold on until God blessed him. We, also, in our wrestling with the Lord must hold on until He blesses us. And He will because He is the same God of Jacob whom we serve. Wrestle if we must, but hold on for our blessing!

Prayer:

Dear Lord, I wrestle with so many things because of the pains of this world. But I hold on until You bless me in this situation. Amen.

Faith Action:

If you have been tussling with God like Jacob, don't let go. Pray every morning, during the day, and night until you receive the peace you need to move forward.

Day 25: God's Questions and Answers

I will question you, and you shall answer me.
Job 38:3

God has a history of asking questions. Adam was asked "Where are you?" Cain was asked, "Where is your brother, Abel?" Moses was asked, "Is the Lord's arm too short?" Elijah was asked, "What are you doing here?" Peter was asked, "Why did you doubt? The disciples were asked, "Who do you say I am?"

What questions is God asking us? When we are going through tough times as Job did, we can forget that God has the questions and answers we need to hear:

God asks: "Who is this that obscures my plans with words without knowledge?" (Job 38:2). Answer: no one, not even the devil. God has a plan even in the most chaotic events in our lives. He has a plan for us to prosper, to give us hope and a future. (Jeremiah 29:11).

God asks: "Where were you when I laid the earth's foundation?" (Job 38:4) Answer: not around. God never takes a vacation. He's everywhere all the time. We may be tempted to believe that God has left us when desolation crowds in on our lives. Yet He said He will never leave nor forsake us. (Hebrews 13:5).

God asks: "Would you discredit my justice?"(Job 40:8). Answer: no. God isn't blind to injustice. We cry out for God's hand to intervene in response to wickedness and yet see nothing changing. However, God promises that He will repay the wrongdoers. (Colossians 3:25).

When we are suffering through a trial, we can draw strength from our faith in God and His perfect plan for our lives, His comforting presence to keep us going, and His enduring justice to repay those who have done wrong.

Prayer:

Dear Lord, help me to trust in your promises to keep me in the time of trouble. I know You are a faithful God to do what You've said in your word. Amen.

Faith Action:

Read through Job 38-40. What question does God ask that intrigues you most? Pray and search the scriptures for answers.

Section 2: Gotta have Friends

"Behold, I have commanded

a widow there to feed you."

1 Kings 17:9

Background Scripture: 1 Kings 17:8-16

Section 2: Gotta Have Friends

Greet the friends, each by name.
3 John 15

Elijah left the brook because God commanded a widow to provide for him. This alone is evidence that God is up to something, because widows and orphans suffered more than anyone else in a famine. Why would a widow have food for him and not some wealthy family? When Elijah arrived in Zarephath, he didn't know exactly from which widow he was to receive provision. He simply asked for water and when she was on her way, he had the audacity to ask for bread as well.

She responded that she didn't have bread. She and her son were going to eat and die after their last morsel of flour. However, hadn't God commanded her to provide for Elijah before his arrival? Why was she prepping her last meal after hearing from God? Yet, she must've suspected that Elijah's word from God was true and in faith, because she prepared his food first. As a result, God provided flour and oil for the duration of the famine. The widow, her son, and Elijah became immediate friends.

God sends His people the right friends at the right time. It's said that friends can be for a reason, a season, or a lifetime. Yet godly friendships have an eternal longevity and our care for each other is richly rewarded by God.

In my difficult transition, I found myself in desperate need for friends. My home needed work to sell, but it was an overwhelming task for me. I didn't have the time, energy, nor skillset to accomplish it by myself. After praying, I sent out an email to friends to help me out. On the designated weekend, I was shocked when over twenty-six people showed up at my home, many of them I didn't know personally. My friends contacted their friends and as a result, my house was ready in a couple of weeks.

This event was deeply humbling for me, and I was moved by the power of love from the body of Christ. There was no way I could've finished the work by myself. Those who participated in the fixing and cleaning up of my home did it with the greatest joy. They saw their sister in need and did what it took to help me in a desperate place.

God blesses us with friends so that we don't have to make this Christian journey all by ourselves. He moves the hearts of our fellow believers to step up when we are in our greatest need. Yet, many of us isolate ourselves from our church friends when we are going through tough times. That's exactly what Satan wants us to do because when two or three of us are gathered together, God is in the midst. (Matthew 18:20)

If we allow ourselves to be vulnerable and accept help from our Christian friends, we may find a renewed sense of hope for the church. More than that, we become friends and helpers of other people in the faith. The twenty-five devotionals in this section are about relationships when you are going through difficult days.

Day 1: Somebody's Watching You

You yourselves are our letter of recommendation.
2 Corinthians 3:2

As professing Christians, we are being watched whether we know it or not. Being a believer doesn't insulate us from the struggles of life whether it's marital separation, financial devastation, debilitating sickness, problems with our children, etc. God allows seasons of trials to grow our faith and draw us closer to Him.

Yet, we have an audience—our family, friends, fellow believers, neighbors, co-workers, classmates, and children. Some are struggling in their life situations and watch us to see if God is real. There may also be those who wait for us to fail in the faith, so that they can feel better about their sins. However, most of our witnesses want us to succeed in the faith in spite of the storms of life.

We are human and have moments where we don't always represent Christ as we should. God gives us grace to seek forgiveness and learn from our mistakes. It's our consistent determination to trust God that gives strength to our testimony. Can we still praise God? Can we still pray in faith? Can we still feed from His word every day?

We can, if we lean on the Lord for strength and wisdom. We handle our lives with grace and it rises as a sweet smelling sacrifice to heaven as well as a witness to those who need to see Jesus in the everyday life. We are on the stage of life with a great audience of potential believers. We aren't perfect, but being perfected in Jesus Christ as we strive to please Him in all things, regardless of our life circumstances.

The steps of faith aren't taken to be noticed by others, rather we take each step believing that God is working everything out for our good. We take one day at a time, trusting in His Holy Word.

Prayer:

Dear Lord, I know that people are watching my walk with You. Help me to live out a strong testimony of your faithfulness and goodness towards me. Amen.

Faith Action:

Who is watching your walk of faith? Ask the Lord to help you witness to them about God's goodness in the midst of trials.

Day 2: Calling it Quits

For the LORD has made the Jordan a boundary
between us and you.
Joshua 22:25

As believers, we are called to love unconditionally and forgive freely just as we have been loved and forgiven by God. Yet there are times when we must release a friendship, relationship, or acquaintance due to their unhealthy influence over our lives. This can be a difficult experience as we often want to be reconciled at all costs.

However, when the reconciliation comes at a spiritual, emotional, or physical cost due to the other parties' resistance to repent or change, it may be time to let it go. In some cases, it may not be a complete disconnect of a relationship especially in the case of families. However, it's sometimes better for us to part ways and continue to intercede for them in prayer.

We must first check our hearts to be sure that we aren't be controlled by our carnal nature more than the Spirit of God. This may require fasting, prayer, focused Bible study, and hard discussions with trusted friends. If there is still the conviction to part ways after doing these things, we can trust in the Lord to give us peace about it.

When we allow the misbehavior of other people to cross the boundaries that God has placed around us, we put ourselves at risk of pleasing people more than God. He has a plan for us that may be hindered by those who fail to respect our boundaries. Jesus has called us to be free to do His will every day without restraints from unhealthy relationships.

Prayer:

Dear Lord, help me recognize the ungodly influences in my life. I pray for the strength and courage to walk away from unhealthy relationships that draw my heart away from You. Amen.

Faith Action:

Is there someone in your life whose influence pulls you away from God? If so, pray for them, but let them go until there is change.

Day 3: God is your Witness

Because the LORD was witness between you and the
wife of your youth.
Malachi 2:14

There are many godly women who stay with a difficult
husband because they want to honor their covenant
with God. These wives may suffer tough times of
feeling unloved and unappreciated by their husbands.
These men may not be mentally or physically abusive,
but rather they may be selfish and without compassion
for their wives.

She can find peace in the midst of a hard marriage
when she turns to God for strength, wisdom, and the
ability to overcome. This is possible because God is an
on-the-scene Witness to every interaction between that
husband and wife. He takes into account every single
word and action that is offensive and without excuse.

Husbands are called to love their wives as Christ loved
the church and gave Himself up for her (Ephesians
5:25). While it isn't easy to always love someone as
Christ does, it's definitely possible to do so in the
power of the Holy Spirit, just as it is possible for a
wife to unconditionally respect her husband in the
power of the Holy Spirit. No one is without excuse,
and God sees everything.

One day every husband and wife will stand before God and give an account of their marriage. She will not give an account of her husband's actions, only hers. Therefore knowing this, a godly wife can stand firm in her faith that God is in control, and He will handle every difficult marital situation. As a Witness to a difficult marriage, the Lord knows exactly how to counsel and comfort wives as they turn to Him for help.

Prayer:

Dear Lord, help me to be the wife that You called me to be. I pray for the power of the Holy Spirit to give me strength and wisdom in this marriage. Amen.

Faith Action:

If you are married to a difficult spouse, begin to seek discernment from God on how to pray for your husband every day. Meditate on Malachi 2:14 to encourage your heart that God sees everything.

Day 4: Not Stuck in the Generational Rut

The faithful God who keeps covenant and steadfast
love…to a thousand generations.
Deuteronomy 7:9

As believers in Jesus Christ, we are not victims of our
parent's decisions or lifestyles. We may have suffered
or are suffering from their choices; however, in Christ
Jesus we are free from those generational bondages.
Many of us have witnessed the multi-generational
issues of alcoholism, drug use, sexual immorality,
theft, lies, anger, and much more. Some of us thought
this was normal, until we matured to see life outside of
the walls of family perceptions.

Many people have escaped their parental examples,
yet without Christ, they will find other ways to fill
those spiritual, emotional, and physical gaps. They
may not practice exactly the same vices of their
parents or grandparents, but they have the same end
results of regret, shame, and guilt.

However, it's not that way for those who give their
lives to Christ. The same power that brought Jesus
back from the dead is available to those who want to
be free from bondages passed down through the
generations. We must first recognize the damage and
desire to be free from it. Afterwards, we seek God's

intervention, wisdom, and knowledge to be free. This happens when we pray, search through His word, and seek godly counsel.

"So if the Son sets you free, you will be free indeed" (John 8:36). You will know the freedom of Christ because He is more powerful than any generational defect of sin. Your freedom may or may not be immediate, but it's coming as long as you stay connected to the Lord. This freedom in Christ isn't just meant for you, but also to other willing family members as well as those whom the Lord puts in your path. Freedom is just the beginning!

Prayer:

Dear Lord, I want to be free of this generational mess and I long for your presence in my life. I pray that You will provide everything I need to walk in the freedom that is available in Christ Jesus. Amen.

Faith Action:

If there is a reoccurring sin or weakness in your family, begin to pray daily for those strongholds to be broken over your family members. Use 2 Corinthians 10:3-6 as a guide.

Day 5: Prickly People

If you love those who love you, what benefit is that to
you?
Luke 6:32

No matter where you live in the world—what job you
have, what neighborhood you live in, or what school
you go to—there is at least one prickly person. This is
someone everyone recognizes as a difficult person.
They don't go along to get along as a practice. As a
matter of fact, they seem to take pride in how they are
set apart from their peers. Your friends, neighbors, and
family members tend to distance themselves from
these prickly people.

But what is our Christ-like response to them? Should
we, like everyone else, distance ourselves? Or should
we see this prickly person as an opportunity to show
the love of Christ?

Distancing ourselves is the easiest and least
complicated action when dealing with a prickly
person. However, we don't know why this person is
difficult to get to know. We also don't know if God
intentionally placed us in the community of this
individual, so that we can be Christ to them.

Prayer is the first and most necessary step in dealing with a difficult person. We begin by setting aside multiple times every day to intercede for this person. By asking God to soften their hearts and minds as well as giving us the wisdom in what to say and do, we are prepping for this opportunity. After praying, we begin to seek the right time to do something special for them. We are staying close to God for wisdom, but we are being watchful and intuitive.

Expect the best, but be prepared for the worst. You may be the recipient of their rejection, criticism, or jeers. They may ridicule your kindness, don't let their reactions derail the Holy Spirit's prompting. You aren't doing this good work because you are good. You are doing it because God is good and you want to please Him in all things.

Prayer:

Dear Lord, You are good and I want to please You by following the lead of the Holy Spirit when dealing with a difficult person. Give me the strength and wisdom to follow through in your name. Amen.

Faith Action:

Write down the name of the prickly person (or people) in your life. Pray Acts 26:18 for them every day.

Day 6: Choose Forgiveness

For if you forgive others their trespasses, your
heavenly Father will also forgive you.
Matthew 6:14

One day I was driving to pick up my daughter and I
was furious about an offense from another person. I
noticed that the sun was going down. "Oh, Lord," I
said, "I don't think my anger is going to be settled
before the sun sets!" This is based on Ephesians 4:26
"Be angry and do not sin; do not let the sun go down
on your anger."

Some people take this verse literally that they need to
settle their anger before nightfall; yet, others interpret
it as giving themselves a set period of time to work the
anger out. The best philosophy is grace to follow
God's word with all our hearts in obedience. We can
pray and ask the Lord for direction and wisdom.

When we are honest about our angry feelings, the
Holy Spirit will begin to deal with our hearts about
choosing forgiveness. He will lead us to recognize that
we choose forgiveness out of obedience to His word
and to forgive just as God has forgiven us.

Choosing forgiveness becomes an act of our will in
respect to God's commandment. We forgive as we are

forgiven; however, our hearts may still feel hurt and anger. We can confess the state of our heart and trust the Holy Spirit to bring healing.

Forgiving someone doesn't take away their consequences for their sins. In fact, if they remain unrepentant—our forgiveness isn't between them and us—rather it's between God and us. The Lord will repay those who do evil. It's our responsibility to obey God's word and trust in Him to settle the differences in His perfect timing.

Prayer:

Dear Lord, I need your Spirit to beckon me more often to choose forgiveness and release my broken heart to You for healing. Keep me tender and obedient to your Word. Amen.

Faith Action:

Is there someone that you haven't forgiven yet? Ask the Lord to help you in this area by drawing close to Him in prayer. He will gently bring you to the right place of forgiveness at the right time.

Day 7: Bring the Joy

The hope of the righteous brings joy.
Proverbs 10:28

Not many of us have the luxury of setting our own work hours. Most of us have to be somewhere for an extended period of time during the week. Some of us love the work we do, while others of us dread it every single day. However, as believers in the Lord Jesus Christ, we have the indwelling power of the Holy Spirit to have joy regardless of the work we have to do.

Those who live without God have times of happiness, but they can't know the joy of the Lord. This is because joy is a gift only for believers. Our joy is in the fruit of the Spirit, and not regulated to what type of career we have.

If we have the gift of joy, we need to share it with those who work around us. While they may not understand it, they will feel our joy when we bring it to work with us. Our joy isn't rooted in whether we get a promotion, raise, or recognition for our work. The joy of the Lord is evident as soon as we arrive at work with our attitude, actions, and words.

We don't have to force our joy, because it happens when we reflect on our lives and how it has changed from darkness to light. As a result, we have unspeakable joy! We remember the good things that God has done for us, even though we didn't deserve it. We meditate on how God has answered our prayers when it seemed impossible for anything to change in our lives. We have joy as a part of our everyday lives when we learn to tap into it.

Prayer:

Dear Lord, help me to remember, reflect, and meditate on your goodness so that joy is always evident in me and to those who work daily around me. Amen.

Faith Action:

Ask the Lord to give you specific things to do every week that will bring joy to the people you work with every day.

Day 8: A House of Peace

It is better to live in a desert land than with a
quarrelsome and fretful woman.
Proverbs 21:19

Those who live in the desert face many perils such as
oppressive heat, unquenchable thirst, painful
sandstorms, and cold nights. However, it's better to
live in the desert than with a discontented woman. We
need to fill our homes with God's peace, rather than
constant turmoil.

We can't control the actions of others, but we can
control our own responses to them. Through the grace
and mercy of God, we can overcome the temptation to
constantly harbor bitterness, anger, and resentment in
our homes. (1 Corinthians 10:13) We can resist
becoming quarrelsome and fretful women by using the
acronym P-E-A-C-E:

P – Pray for God's help and strength. Many of us rely
first on ourselves or we call on friends to deal with the
mess in our homes. We can call on God first to calm
our hearts and give us wisdom.

E – Expect God to move on our behalf. Even if we are
dependent on the actions of others, we are completely
dependent on God to move mountains for us.

A – Act as though today was our last day on earth. Do we want our family to remember us as a discontented, angry people? Or could their memory of us be someone who trusted in God even in incredibly difficult situations.

C – Close the door of our mind to the suggestions of the devil. Satan will take advantage of a situation to bring unclean and sinful thoughts to our mind. Be reactive and resist evil thoughts with the word of God.

E – Elevate our conversations to be edifying, encouraging, and loving to our family members. God will give us the right words to say if we ask Him even in the midst of a conversation.

As we follow the way of P-E-A-C-E, God will make our homes a peaceful habitation, where everyone who lives and visits can sense the presence of the Spirit.

Prayer:

Dear Lord, without your help my house will be a desert of discontentment and discord. I pray for your peace and presence to fill my home. Amen.

Faith Action:

Do you live in a house of peace? Ask the Holy Spirit to awaken your heart to make your home a house of peace and not friction.

Day 9: A Love that Lasts

For his steadfast love endures forever.
Psalm 136:26

When we are hurt by those who are closest to us, there is the temptation to feel like we are unloved. Some of us have been turned away and forsaken by our relatives, spouses, and children. In those times, the hurt is more than we could ever express in words. Yet, we are loved most intensely by God, whether we feel it or not.

God loved us so much that He sent His one and only Son to die, so that we could have eternal life with Him. He loves us so much that He desires the best for us in every way. He loves us so much that He forgives every single sin we have committed and cleanses us from all unrighteousness. He loves us so much that He gives us new grace and mercy every single day.

Because of His love for us, we don't have to live burden down with guilt, fear, or shame. His love encompasses us so that we are free to be everything that He created us to be. We are overcomers, victorious over sin, new creations, a royal priesthood, and children of the Creator because of God's love for each one of us.

There is nothing that can ever separate us from the love of God. Paul wrote it best in Romans 8:35, 38-39 "Shall tribulation, or distress, or persecution, or famine, or nakedness, or danger, or sword?...neither death nor life, nor angels nor rulers, nor things present nor things to come, nor powers, nor height nor depth, nor anything else in all creation, will be able to separate us from the love of God in Christ Jesus our Lord." We are secure in God's love that lasts forever!

Prayer:

Dear Lord, let me know the depth of your love for me every day so that I don't believe the lies of the enemy. Amen.

Faith Action:

Make a list of everything listed in Romans 8:35-39 that can't separate you from God's love. Every time you struggle with feeling unloved, remember how there's nothing that can separate you from His love.

Day 10: You are Worth It!

Because you are precious in my eyes, and honored,
and I love you.
Isaiah 43:3

Anyone who's ever been a codependent almost always struggles with their self-worth. Because of this struggle, there is a tendency to settle for less than God's best, especially when it comes to our relationships. Instead of finding our value in God, we find it in trying to please someone else. These relationships rarely end well.

God doesn't want us to settle for unhealthy relationships, in order to feel good about ourselves. He wants us to be whole and complete in Jesus Christ first, so that we can be free to do His will and clearly hear God's voice. When we believe the satanic lie that we aren't good enough or worth the trouble, our hearts become breeding ground for being manipulated and controlled by other people. We will go to all sorts of trouble to be loved and accepted by those who don't really love us.

The only true cure for this codependency lifestyle is a total spiritual makeover. It's accepting what God says about us and rejecting the lies of the enemy without doubt nor hesitation. It may not happen overnight, but with due diligence in the memorization and application of God's word, we can be completely changed from the inside out.

Knowing that we are a new creation (2 Corinthians 5:17), bought with a price (1 Corinthians 7:23), accepted (Romans 14:18), loved (1 John 4:10), precious (1 Peter 3:4), and chosen (1 Peter 2:4), will give us the confidence to move forward.

There will be resistance from those who desire us to stay in the place of codependency, but we must press past the old mindset of low self-worth and rise to the power given by God through His word.

Prayer:

Dear Lord, I've made so many mistakes in being codependent. Help me to step up and out of old patterns of thinking and become everything You called me to be in Christ Jesus. Amen.

Faith Action:

Seek God's discernment to know if you are a codependent. If so, trust in His hand to show you clear direction from this bondage.

Day 11: A Simple Thank You

And be thankful.
Colossians 3:15

When Jesus was on His way to Jerusalem, ten men with leprosy cried out to Him for healing. Jesus commanded them to show themselves to the priest and as they were leaving, they were miraculously healed. Yet only one of the men (a Samaritan) turned back and thanked Jesus. Jesus asked, "Were not ten cleansed? Where are the nine? Was no one found to return and give praise to God except this foreigner?" (Luke 17:17-18)

What did the other former lepers do after showing themselves to the priest? Did they return to their families? Did they go back to their former homes and work? Perhaps ten days or years later they remembered to themselves and said, *"Oh yeah! Thank you Jesus!"*

When an executive of a corporation takes a moment to express gratefulness to the maintenance worker changing a light bulb, it gives this person a renewed sense of belonging and recognition for their work. When a parent thanks their son or daughter for cleaning their room, it speaks to the heart of the child that their efforts are appreciated. Likewise, when a son or daughter thanks their parents for what was done for them, a mom or dad smiles inside.

Some may feel that it's unnecessary to thank someone for doing what they are supposed to do. Yet a spirit of thankfulness should mark us in all of our relationships, because we reap God's benefits every single day whether we thank Him or not. We don't always remember to thank Him and He still blesses us. As believers we can be the chief encouragers in our home, at school, at work, and in our community with a simple 'thank you'.

Prayer:

Dear Lord, thank You for everything You have done and continue to do for me. Forgive me for the times I've been like the nine lepers and didn't return to express my gratefulness. Amen.

Faith Action:

Have a Thankful Thursday every week for your family and you to share with each other what things God has given you.

Day 12: A Trophy Wife

An excellent wife is the crown of her husband.
Proverbs 12:4

In the eyes of the world, Esther would be considered a trophy wife of King Ahasuerus. She was taken from her uncle's home because of her beauty. Esther was included with seven other attractive young women to be subjected to a year of cosmetics and perfumes in preparation for one night with the king. He would choose one of them to be the next queen. Those not chosen would become a part of the king's harem for the rest of their lives.

Esther was loved and chosen by the king. Her story could've ended there, but God had a purpose and plan for her. She was more than just a trophy wife because it was "such a time as this" in which her fasting, praying, and interceding saved the Jews from annihilation.

Just like Esther, many Christian women believers are married to unbelieving or carnal Christian husbands. Sometimes it's easy to feel like praying, fasting, and serving their husbands are all in vain. However, God hears the prayers of a praying wife, and she is a trophy or crown to her husband, even if he doesn't realize it.

While a trophy wife could be considered a derogatory term, a praying wife is more than a trophy, she is the lifeline for the family. God's word teaches that if an unbelieving husband is willing to remain with his believing wife, she may win him over to the Lord. It may be difficult at times; however, God sees and knows her. He will sustain and strengthen her faith to change her husband's heart just as He used Esther to rescue an entire nation.

Prayer:

Dear Lord, help me to be strong and stand in the gap for my unbelieving husband. I know that there's nothing too hard for You. Give me the wisdom on how to pray. Amen.

Faith Action:

Find a prayer book that is specifically related to marriage. Commit to praying through that book for your husband every day.

Day 13: Everyone needs a Nathan

Nathan said to David, "You are the man!"
2 Samuel 12:7

When David committed adultery with Bathsheba, it seemed like he would get away with it. After he arranged for her husband's death, David married Bathsheba and they enjoyed their new child together. The Bible has no record of anyone chastising David for his sin. The servants who sent for Bathsheba didn't say anything. The general who put Bathsheba's husband in a place where he would be killed in battle said nothing. However, there was a prophet of God who wouldn't let David get away with his sin.

Nathan was wise in his approach to David, he didn't come right out and challenge David's sin. Instead, he told a story about a man who loved his ewe lamb and how a rich man (with many flocks and herds) selfishly slaughtered the poor man's beloved lamb in order to entertain company. David was outraged and called for the rich man's death. In response, Nathan said to David, "You are the man!"

While we may not have done the same sins as David, we have fallen short and needed correction from someone close to us. We need a Nathan to remind us that God has blessed us with many blessings so we don't covet. We need a Nathan to encourage us to live righteous and pure lives that are untainted by worldly living. We need a Nathan so our hearts don't become full of pride and selfishness because of our spiritual or financial increase.

Being an active part of the body of Christ gives us much exposure. We are exposed of our own shortcomings as well as those of other people. A true Nathan in our lives won't look to judge us too harshly or quickly, because they are always aware of their own faults. Yet, they love us too much to let us wander in the darkness of sin.

Prayer:

Dear Lord, I pray for people in my life who will encourage me to keep my eyes on Christ and not the things of this world. Amen.

Faith Action:

Do you have a "Nathan" in your life? If not, pray and ask the Lord to send a godly friend who will encourage your walk in Christ.

Day 14: Need a Man?

You will call me 'My Husband'.
Hosea 2:16

These days almost every popular TV show or movie will have a love scene. Young women are duped daily with these shows and music to believe that they need a man in order for everything to be right in the world. While there's a place for true love and marriage for those who desire it, it's not what is central to every single woman's life.

A Christian woman can have a life without a man, without a boyfriend, without a husband. It's not God's will that His single daughters sit around all day waiting for a man to rescue them from their lives. Instead, God wants His daughters to be actively engaged in life and living with eternity on their minds every day.

If she desires to be married one day, God will want her to be with someone who is compatible in the faith and with her destiny as a wife. He will provide a good man as she waits patiently on God, not passively, but proactively involved in ministry and building the kingdom of heaven. When her earthly husband does come around, he will find a whole woman in which to build a good life. A good Christian man is seeking out someone he can partner with, and not someone whom he can save from a boring life.

While she waits, the Lord is her Husband and He will meet all of her spiritual, emotional, and physical needs. Anyone who needs a man can look to the Lord, and He will take care of them. The Lord longs for single women to direct their attention to Him. God knows everything about their needs and will do whatever it takes to keep them on the right journey.

Prayer:

Dear Lord, give me to desire You more than anyone else. I pray for strength when I feel weak in my faith in You. Amen.

Faith Action:

Write out Isaiah 54:5 on an index card and keep it on a bathroom mirror to remind yourself every day about how God will meet all your needs.

Day 15: When People Leave You

For Demas, in love with this present world, has
deserted me.
2 Timothy 4:10

It's tough when a close friend leaves us, especially if we never really had a chance to understand the reason for their departure. Our recovery from the loss depends on the length of time of the friendship. A longer, more intimate relationship will take more time than a shorter one. It's important for us to allow the Spirit of God to comfort and encourage us for these times.

We can spend too much time trying to figure out what went wrong and not enough time seeking out God's insight. The Lord will allow some friendships to end, especially if they aren't helpful to us growing closer to Him. If we are the unhealthy part of it, He will allow relationships to break. In Paul's case, Demas left him because his love for the world was greater than his love for God. Whatever the reason, the loss of a close companion is painful.

Rejection from those who've left us can be overcome. We will eventually find ourselves removed emotionally from the loss and able to recuperate. Jesus was in close and intimate connection with the disciples. Yet, when He needed them most, every single one of them abandoned him. Even so, Jesus received them back after the resurrection.

The Lord is a comfort to those who find themselves friendless because He knows what it feels like. He uses the gaping wound in our hearts to bring us closer to Him. We learn to find Jesus Christ as a friend that is closer than any relative. We find Him to be a private and trusted Confidante who knows our heart and intentions. As a result of this friendship, we forgive those who've hurt us and move on towards other friendships that are balanced and healthy.

Prayer:

Dear Lord, my loss of this friend is hard to overcome. I pray for your peace and comfort to forgive and move on with the life You've called me to live. Amen.

Faith Action:

Do you have a friend who has abandoned you? Ask the Lord for peace and pray for them as the Spirit leads us.

Day 16: Lord, I want Friends

A friend loves at all times, and a brother is born for
adversity.
Proverbs 17:17

Friends are those we can be ourselves around, and they
will love us with all of our faults. They make us feel
loved and they are there for us, when times get tough.
These are the type of friends who stick around when
everyone else has forgotten about us and our struggles.

The problem for many of us is that we've had a hard
time finding those type of friends. We've been hurt by
those who were close to us, and therefore we struggle
with trusting people. Or we get tired of the cliques that
only result in isolation or dependency. Sometimes it's
difficult to find friends, because we are so busy that
we find ourselves alone.

Whatever the reason for our lack of friendships, we
still have that inner desire for connection on a deeper
level. The Lord has created in each of us a desire for
relationships, in addition to our relationship with Him.
We need Christian friendships for fellowship,
accountability, and opportunity.

Fellowship with other believers causes us to laugh at
ourselves and recognize that we are not alone in our

struggles in the faith. The accountability of friendships helps us to keep our standards high in the Lord so that we don't fall into sin or unhealthy relationships. The opportunity of friendships allows us to serve and pray for each other through the difficult days, and celebrate with each other the joyous times.

We pray for God's guidance for friends who will stretch our faith in the Lord, without the temptations to give more opportunity for the sinful nature. In this time of waiting, we must be patient and alert for God to lead us to the right people. We also need to let go of any preconceptions of what our friends will look like or act like, because God looks at the heart more than the outside appearances.

Prayer:

Dear Lord, I pray for good friends in the faith. Help me to be the friend that You've called me to be for them as well. Amen.

Faith Action:

Ask the Lord to show you friends in places you haven't considered before.

Day 17: Unfailing Love

Love never ends.
1 Corinthians 13:8

Marriage is a wonderful gift from God. It's a bond that is meant to last until death. We live in a world where people marry for money, reputation, status, or just because everyone else is doing it. However, in God's eyes, marriage is a covenant for life unless there is adultery, an unbelieving spouse leaves, or death. Couples who want to get married need lots of time for prayer, study of God's word, and godly counsel before their commitment.

Unconditional love in a marriage can survive regardless of tough times. This life will bring many trials and troubles that will threaten a marriage. When the husband and wife are united through the power of God, they will together overcome great difficulties and remain committed to each other for life.

Through the grace and mercy of God, believers experience the agape or unconditional love of Christ. This agape love is a necessity in order to remain married for life, because there will be times when a spouse can seem unlovable. As followers of Jesus Christ, we all have our weaknesses and in marriage, the weaknesses are most apparent to the spouse. Yet, love never fails, even when a husband or wife fails. It will cover them in the enduring love of God.

In order for this agape love to remain throughout the marriage, there has to be an effort to show this love. As couples grow together in years, it's easy to take each other for granted. It's important to ask the Holy Spirit to refresh your hearts for each other, so that you don't succumb to the temptations of the sinful nature. There is power from God to bring a renewed and passionate love for each other. God wants Christian couples to reflect His love for each other.

Prayer:

Dear Lord, forgive me for the times I didn't show agape love to my spouse. Reignite unconditional love in our marriage. Amen.

Faith Action:

Through God's grace and strength, do something every day that is an act of agape love to your spouse.

Day 18: Make your Mark

Among whom you shine as lights in the world.
Philippians 2:15

Many believers struggle with the day-to-day requirements of their work responsibilities; however, none of us are randomly placed where we work. God has strategically positioned us where He can most effectively use our gifts for the building of the kingdom, regardless of our work environment.

If our work doesn't allow for many opportunities for promotions or raises, we can be tempted to become discontent. If we have discord on the job due to a difficult boss or coworkers, our attitude can lead to discouragement. However, we are created for God's purpose and our identity isn't limited to the work we do. Since we work for the Lord and not for our boss, there can be peace knowing that our real boss is Jesus Christ. Our true boss wants us to work towards greater peace, accomplishment, and success in our lives; therefore, we are encouraged to press forward each and every day doing our best.

God expects His people to leave a positive mark on their place of employment. We aren't just existing from paycheck to paycheck, we are a part of His kingdom agenda, regardless of where we work.

Because we showed up for work, there needs to be a positive impact from our presence. Even in the worst work environments, we can pray for the salvation of our bosses and co-workers. We can pray for God's peace and presence to infiltrate the building. We can pray for opportunities to share the gospel or help someone through a difficult situation. Believers who follow God with all their hearts can't help, but leave the mark of Jesus Christ wherever they work.

Prayer:

Dear Lord, I want to leave the mark of Jesus Christ at my job every day. I pray for wisdom and insight to do this with integrity and courage. Amen.

Faith Action:

Who can you encourage in the workplace? Begin to seek out opportunities to leave a positive mark in your place of employment by showing grace and mercy to those God places in your path.

Day 19: Releasing Painful People

Whom I have handed over to Satan.
1 Timothy 1:20

How long do we tarry with painful people? Many of us have prayed earnestly for people who remain unrepentant and stubbornly attached to wickedness. We keep giving them opportunities to change, and they cast away our acts of kindness.

Because of our love, we continue to give grace and mercy in hopes that they will change. However, what if God is leading us to release them to the devil for their discipline? Do we have the courage to do this?

In the Corinthian church, there was a man who was having sexual relations with his father's wife. Even in the pagan culture of Corinth—this was an unacceptable and flagrant act of immorality. Paul's instruction to the leaders of the church was "to deliver this man to Satan for the destruction of the sinful nature, so that his spirit may be saved in the day of the Lord" (1 Corinthians 5:5).

Paul's reasoning for this severe discipline was to protect that church from allowing the seed of sexual immorality to take root. Later, in 2 Corinthians 2:7-8, we learn of the man's repentance and Paul admonished the church "to forgive and comfort him, or he may be overwhelmed by excessive sorrow...reaffirm your love for him."

It will never be easy to release those we love to be disciplined by Satan. We know that our enemy seeks to do great harm to them because he never stops seeking opportunities to kill, steal, and destroy. However, doing so in faith, prayer, and trusting in God can result in this person having a change of heart. We don't release them in a spirit of anger, bitterness, nor revenge. We release them to Satan, so that even if their bodies are destroyed, their spirits can be saved through Christ.

Prayer:

Dear Lord, you know how I've labored in prayer for my loved one. Help me to release them in order that they may know You and receive eternal life. Amen.

Faith Action:

Put aside time every day to pray for wisdom to release painful people from your life.

Day 20: Sloppy Agape

Let all that you do be done in love.
1 Corinthians 16:14

There are many people who confess to be Christians, but their words and actions seem to contradict what the Bible teaches. It's evident in their lack of love to other people, especially unbelievers. It's much easier to love those who love us, than it is to love those who hate us, hate our God, and hate our convictions. Yet, sloppy agape love repels more people from the cross than anything else we do.

This sloppy agape love is most evident when we are confronted with the realities of a culture which distorts the truth of God to accommodate their sinful desires. We are tempted to not love others, because their choices and lifestyles are in direct conflict to the teachings of the Bible. Yet, we are in this world and not of the world. The world loves those who love them and hates those who hate them. However, it's different for us as believers, we love those who hate us because of the genuine concern for their souls.

It's not always easy to show the unconditional love of Christ. Many people have set themselves as enemies of the cross and will do whatever it takes to destroy those who love God. Yet, the agape love of God will give us discernment and wisdom when dealing with those who are deceived by the evil one. We can pray and meditate in God's word to receive power from the Holy Spirit to love unconditionally.

When we are at home, work, school, or in our communities, we can demonstrate the love of Christ in such a way that they know we are different. Agape love is unconditional, and we can genuinely reflect this love regardless of the choices of other people.

Prayer:

Dear Lord, please forgive me for the times I've been showing sloppy agape love to those who hate the cause of Christ. Fill me with your Holy Spirit to love all people at all times with my words and actions. Amen.

Faith Action:

Ask the Lord to reveal those people you can show genuine agape love towards every day.

Day 21: The Blame Game

The woman whom you gave to be with me.
Genesis 3:12

When God asked Adam about the tree of knowledge of good and evil, Adam's response was not, "Yes, God. I ate of the tree that you told me not to eat." Instead Adam began with "The woman who you gave to be with me..." Blame. Blame. Blame. Eve was no better when she was asked; her response was "The serpent deceived me..." Blame. Blame. Blame. God didn't even ask Satan any questions. Wonder who he would blame? Perhaps he would say, "Well if you never created me..."

It's in our sinful nature to want someone else to shoulder the blame for what we've done. It's not us. It's our spouses, parents, kids, bosses, neighbors, co-workers, etc. Why is it so difficult for us to face our wrong instead of passing it off to other people? The next time we feel tempted to blame someone else, let's examine our hearts with the following questions using the acronym B-L-A-M-E:

B – Be honest with our true intentions in the situation. What role did we play with our own free will?

L – Let go of our desire to look good in front of people. Is our pride keeping us from admitting our sin?

A – Ask close family members and friends to be truthful with what they see as our role in the situation. Do we receive their feedback with humility, or are we deflecting it with excuses?

M – Make sure to confess our sins against other people. Can we genuinely confess our sins and seek forgiveness from someone else?

E – Expect the Holy Spirit to lead us into all truth. Have we let go of excuses and invited the Spirit to lead us toward repentance?

Every one of us has struggled with the blame game, yet as we mature in the Spirit, we will put away childish excuses and step up to our own responsibility.

Prayer:

Dear Lord, I confess my sin of playing the blame game. I seek your forgiveness and cleansing from unrighteousness. Amen.

Faith Action:

Next time you are tempted to blame someone...take a deep breath and ask God for insight to see the situation just as He does.

Day 22: How deep is your Love?

Above all, keep loving one another earnestly.
1 Peter 4:8

In 1977, the disco group, Bee Gees, released a song about how deep is the love of a person in the relationship. While it describes a love that has expectations, there is the recognition that this love continually goes away. The world has the ability to express the depth of expected love; however, it can't compete with the unconditional love of God for His children and His children's love for one another.

We are called to love each other deeply in Christ. This type of love is difficult, if not impossible, to express on our own. Many of us are conditioned to love those who love us. We aren't skilled in the art of loving those who are difficult to love, who may mistreat us, or who may cause us to feel weary with helping them. The temptation to avoid, ignore, and resist those who aren't loving comes much easier than unconditional love of God.

Through the presence of the Holy Spirit, we are given the ability to love unconditionally (Romans 5:5). To love one another earnestly is to go deeper than surface love. It's the type of love that will have us get up early or stay up late praying for each other. It's the type of love that helps a grieving believer long after the funeral. It's the type of love that steps up to help a young struggling mother or a lonely elderly widow. It's the type of love that patiently disciples a new believer in Christ.

Each of us may need to ask ourselves "how deep is our love really?" Are we more conditioned to express love to those who are easier to love and serve? Or do we stay close to the heart of God to discern those who may be needy for our agape love?

Prayer:

Dear Lord, I confess that my love can be conditional at times. I pray for You to fill my heart with agape love of Christ for my brothers and sisters in the Lord.

Faith Action:

Write a list of names of people that you can show love to and ask God to give you creative ways to express that love to each of them.

Day 23: To Bless or Impress

I will bless you...so that you will be a blessing.
Genesis 12:2

In the holiday season, and with any celebrations, many of us find ourselves hosting guests in our homes. It can be a busy and frustrating task to get our homes ready, food prepared, and families in line to entertain. Sometimes it's easy for us to get caught up in trying to impress our company instead of being a blessing to them. We can be a blessing if we use these five Biblical strategies for entertaining guests using the acronym B-L-E-S-S:

B - Be Focused on God's Purpose (Isaiah 55:6)

While we may be preoccupied by the smudge on the wall, our guests may be struggling with a difficult marriage, a wayward child, or bankruptcy. The immaculate state of our homes has diminished value compared to meeting the spiritual or emotional needs of our guests.

L - Let Go of Unrealistic Expectations (Philippians 4:11)

Waiting until our houses are picture perfect could translate into "no guests at all." A spirit of contentment can nurture a renewed thankfulness for the opportunity to express hospitality.

E - Encourage Family Participation (Proverbs 22:6)

Assigning children duties, such as taking coats or setting the table, helps train them in the role of hospitality. As they take an active involvement in hosting and preparing for company (even if it isn't as perfect as mom does it), they have a vested interest in making the evening as pleasant as possible.

S - Simplify…Simplify…Simplify (Ecclesiastes 9:10)

When we simplify our expectations, our anxieties are lessened by keeping preparations simple. The art of cultivating and maintaining good relationships is far more rewarding than an extravagant menu.

S – Season our Homes with God's Presence (Matthew 5:13)

Our hospitality gives the family an opportunity to be salt and light to guests. As we seek to be a blessing to others, our home will stand out not for its external beauty, but as lighthouse in a lost and fallen world.

Prayer:

Dear Lord, help me to be mindful of being a blessing to those You send to my home. Give me how to express a spirit of contentment and thankfulness to my guests. Amen.

Faith Action:

Plan your next gathering of family and friends with the focus of blessing them and giving them an opportunity to be a blessing to someone else.

Day 24: Spinach in the Teeth

Faithful are the wounds of a friend; profuse are the
kisses of an enemy.
Proverbs 27:6

Have you ever had spinach (or some other unsightly
food) in your teeth, and no one told you about it? Or
perhaps your skirt was not quite pulled down or your
dress not zipped up all the way? Those are the times
you wish that someone had told you, instead of letting
you walk around all day looking unsightly.

A good friend will tell you the truth about yourself,
even if it might be a little awkward in the delivery.
They care enough about you, and they are confident
that you will do the same for them as well. Sometimes
the "spinach in the teeth" isn't something that is
physically misplaced about you. It may be that you
talk too much, on the verge of being a gossip. Or
perhaps, you are driving people away because you've
become overly sensitive. Whatever the reason, a
trusted friend will tell you the truth about yourself.

What we must embrace is that the "wounds of a friend
can be trusted". Those who don't love us won't tell us
the truth about ourselves. They are content to let us
walk around with all of our weaknesses and faults on

display for everyone to see. By doing so, they can feel superior to us.

However, a friend speaks the truth in love without holding back. They take into account that they also have weaknesses and want us to help them out as well. These conversations aren't easy, but necessary for friendships to grow deeper and more meaningful. There is a great connection and bond between friends who feel the freedom to share the truth with each other.

Prayer:

Dear Lord, help me to speak the truth in love to my close family and friends. Help me to also to be open to their sharing truth with me. Amen.

Faith Action:

If God has placed a friend who needs correction on your mind, pray for wisdom on how to help them gently.

Day 25: When God is your Friend

Shall I hide from Abraham what I am about to do?
Genesis 18:17

After sharing the wonderful news of Abraham and
Sarah's upcoming pregnancy and birth of their son,
God asked if He should hide his plan to destroy
Sodom and Gomorrah. Why would the God of the
universe feel compelled to share this with a mere
human? Abraham was called a friend of God (James
2:23). This is significant because of what friendships
tend to entail—trust, transparency, love, etc.

As God's friend, Abraham was able to take part in a
conversation with God on His impending judgment on
two great cities. Abraham immediately responded with
requests of intercession for the people. He bravely
kept asking God for mercy, even if there were only ten
people in the city who were righteous. God promised
to relent His judgment if this were true. Yet, even
though ten people weren't found, God graciously
delivered Abraham's nephew Lot and his family from
certain destruction.

As heirs of Abraham, we can build a friendship with
God that will be evident in our growing faith in Him.
Abraham became a friend of God because he believed
in His promise for a child, even though his own body

Grace is a gift that rescues us from stressing and worrying about how things are going to work out. His power is revealed in grace as we accomplish everything we set out to do with a different focus of pleasing God. His grace reins us in from taking the full credit for completed work and accomplishments. We know there was no way anything was done, unless God's grace allowed it. By embracing the grace, we are set free from seeking accolades from others, and instead we are overwhelmingly grateful to the God who strengthens us.

Prayer:

Dear Lord, I pray for the grace to accomplish the tasks that are in front of me today. Help me to remember to pause and seek out your grace. Amen.

Faith Action:

Where do you need to experience God's grace the most? Next time you feel stressed, ask God for the grace to get through it.

Day 2: God's Plans are better than my Plans

For I know the plans I have for you.
Jeremiah 29:11

Some of us are good planners. We have vacations laid out to detail so that there are no sudden surprises or disappointments. Many of us have our retirement plans in order, so that we can relax in our golden years without the stress of working every day. Young couples also make plans to get married, have kids, buy a home, etc.

However, life doesn't always fit into our plans. Loved ones get sick and die before we had a chance to say goodbye. Infertility happens to many couples, who long to raise children in the Lord. Retirements aren't planned always to include a divorce or financial ruin because of financial mismanagement. What are we supposed to do when things don't always go the way we desired for ourselves or family?

We don't always get to choose our life journey. The Lord has a plan for every single one of His children. His plan includes the good and bad of this world. Just because we become Christians doesn't mean that our lives are insulated from disappointments or tragedies. For example, many believers around the world suffer because they refuse to deny Jesus Christ as Lord.

The beauty of having a relationship with Jesus Christ is that we know that He is in control of our lives, and that He will never leave nor forsake us. When we have struggles in this life, just knowing that God has a plan, gives us hope for the future. We aren't abandoned just because things are going badly, rather we cling to the cross even more and increase our dependency on the Lord. His plans for us are good, even when it gets tough.

Prayer:

Dear Lord, I know that your plans for my life are better than mine. Help me to trust You with my life plan and to choose faith over fear when times get hard. Amen.

Faith Action:

Draw a short time line of your life marking significant events. In a different color, write in the different ways that God was a part of those times.

Day 3: Inadvertent God-Intersections

The heart of man plans his way, but the LORD
establishes his steps.
Proverbs 16:9

Have you had the experience of unexpectedly crossing paths with someone and before you knew it, there was a God moment? It might be that the person is open and responsive to hearing the gospel. Or perhaps you run into a friend who is going through a difficult situation and you were just the person that they needed to connect with.

Our intersections may be inadvertent and unplanned on our part; however, God knows the right timing for our personal connections. This is why it is important for us to start our day with prayers and scripture reading. We never know who we might run into that day and their need for that word from God.

We aren't chosen because we are the most theologically sound or spiritually mature. Rather, we are chosen because God knows that our experience and knowledge of Him can be beneficial to those He sends our way. God knows the thoughts of all people and He knows just the right person to represent Jesus Christ.

In those moments, we will have two simultaneous discussions: one with the person as we listen to them and one with God as we are asking Him for wisdom and discernment on what to say. The Holy Spirit will prompt us in the right direction, as we learn to hear His voice and respond in obedience.

People can see that we are the walking evidence of the Bible by what we say and how we live.

It's important that we remain in right relationship with God, and not live a carnal lifestyle that will contradict what we say. Our lives are a witness of God's grace, presence, and influence.

Prayer:

Dear Lord, give me the desire to be a living epistle to those You send my way. I need to hear your voice in my heart to speak the right words of encouragement and strength. Amen.

Faith Action:

Ask God to give you wisdom and discernment on what to say. Look for opportunities to have inadvertent God-intersections.

Day 4: Favor is not Fair

Let the favor of the Lord our God rest on us.
Psalm 90:17

Abraham had the favor of God on his life when he was called to go to an unknown land, and become the father of many nations.

Jacob had the favor of God on his life when he left his homeland, and became more successful than his father-in-law.

Joseph had the favor of God when he was taken as a slave, to become second leader over Potiphar's home (until he was falsely accused), second leader of the prisoners, and eventually second in command over the nation of Egypt.

Moses had the favor of God when he was spared being killed as a baby, and rose up to lead the Israelites to the Promised Land.

David had the favor of God when he rose up from being a young unknown shepherd boy to one of the greatest kings of Israel, and his seed being chosen as the Messiah of the world.

will rise in victory and praise to God for His deliverance.

This process will ebb and flow as we may be prone to unsteadiness due to the duration and severity of our trials. We will learn to level set ourselves as long as we consistently return to the Rock of our salvation for restoration. Our down moments won't define our faith, because we will experience God's comfort and support.

Prayer:

Dear Lord, I long to have that peace that passes all understanding through this difficult time. Help me to cling to your power in the Spirit to rest in your plan for my life. Amen.

Faith Action:

Next time you are tempted to pace about your problems, imagine dropping each one of them off at the foot of the cross.

Day 9: Favor on the Job

But the LORD was with Joseph…and gave him favor.
Genesis 39:21

Joseph went through an incredible culture shock at a young age. He was accustomed to being under the watchful care of his father, when suddenly Joseph was thrown in a pit by his own brothers. Yet, Joseph held on to what he was taught about God. He worked diligently for Potiphar and was made second in charge. After being unjustly accused of rape by Potiphar's wife, Joseph found favor with the jailer. Regardless of where he lived or what he did, God's favor was on him.

Up until Joseph was made second in command over all Egypt, he was probably treated unfairly or perhaps other workers became jealous of him because of his success (just like his brothers). Yet, the Lord rose Joseph from a slave and prisoner to a position of high honor.

Just like Joseph, we need the favor of God on our jobs, regardless of our work environment. Sometimes it may be difficult, especially for those of us who work for unfair bosses. Yet God's favor is greater than man's favor. We don't have to work hard to get people to like us, we work hard for the Lord, and expect Him to take care of us everywhere we work.

The favor of God is greater than any CEO of the most successful corporations. We serve the King of kings and Lord of lords over the whole earth. Every believer belongs to Him, and He will reward our faithfulness even in times of difficulty on the job. Our responsibility is to work hard and resist the temptation of looking towards man instead of God. The Lord knows how to put us in the right place at the right time.

Prayer:

Dear Lord, I pray for your favor over me at my job every day. I ask for grace to see the many opportunities You give me to be light and salt to my coworkers. Amen.

Faith Action:

Ask the Lord for His favor in a specific area at your job, that you might represent the kingdom of God.

Day 10: Freedom of Exposure

I heard you in the garden, and I was afraid because I
was naked; so I hid.
Genesis 3:10

The social media is off the chart with exposed issues
of politicians and celebrities. Some people spent a lot
of money covering up present and/or past sins. The
outcry on these situations is a mixture of
understanding and condemnation. Our tendency as
human beings is to do everything we can to keep our
sins hidden away; however, there can be grace and
freedom in the exposure of sin.

When we attempt to hide our sins, we remain in
darkness and isolated from God and the fellowship of
other believers. Yet, if we confess our faults to God
and one another, we can find grace to help in our time
of need. The exposure of our sins will most likely have
consequences that we would like to avoid. However,
God uses our consequences to drive us closer to Him
and His word. He also uses our situations as an
opportunity to witness, and help others to avoid our
same mistakes.

The reality is that we can never hide from God
because He is everywhere and knows everything. As
believers of God, we will be disciplined for our sinful

actions. God doesn't discipline us because He finds pleasure in it, He disciplines us because of His unconditional love for us. The Lord wants us to succeed in this life journey that He has given us. We can't grow in our relationship with Him if we avoid dealing with our sins.

The exposure of sins helps us to move forward and learn to overcome obstacles to our faith. While the discipline of our sins isn't fun, we gain so much more as we are humbled and rebuilt in our firm conviction to live righteously in Christ. When our sins are exposed, we need to resist the temptation to run away from Jesus. Instead we must run straight towards Him, fall on our faces, and receive His unfailing love, grace, and mercy.

Prayer:

Dear Lord, I need your forgiveness for my sins. I pray for your cleansing and healing from my brokenness.

Faith Action:

Ask the Lord to reveal any unconfessed sin in your life. Repent and be made whole in Him.

Day 11: Happy every Day!

This is the day that the LORD has made.
Psalm 118:24

At the end of every work week, I'm usually greeted by other colleagues with "Happy Friday!" It used to catch me off guard because the weekends are usually a mess of activities for me. I may not have to go into the workplace, but I have writing, kid's activities, grocery shopping, house cleaning, and ministry responsibilities. So, even though I may not have to go into the office, I'm still running all over the place.

In order to keep myself from being stressed, I decided to make every day a happy day to stay focused and positive both at home and work. For me, it's Happy Monday, Happy Tuesday, Happy Wednesday, etc. There's a great tendency to work all week looking for that golden day of rest. Although I still rest more on the weekend even with my responsibilities, I recognize that not one day is promised to me. I have to make the most of every day, because life isn't guaranteed to continue until the weekend.

How many people prepared for work the night before by laying out their clothes, packing a lunch, or checking their emails, but they didn't wake up for work because their time was up? They may have had good intentions, but their numbers of days had reached its conclusion. If there is breathe in our bodies and strength to get up and on with our day...rejoice!

Every day is a happy day in the Lord. He gives us strength when we feel weak, He comforts us when we feel alone, and He enables through His power to be good workers on our jobs. We have a choice to either live every day as though it was our last or to mindlessly work the week until we can say "Happy Friday!" That is if we make it to Friday...

Prayer:

Dear Lord, help me to appreciate every day as a gift from You. I need your presence and power of my life to work well in my home, workplace, and community. Amen.

Faith Action:

Begin greeting your family, friends, and co-workers with a renewed sense of joy for every day God has given you.

Day 12: Intentional not Accidental

Why, even the hairs of your head are all numbered.
Luke 12:7

Sometimes it's hard to believe that every event in our lives is orchestrated by God. Tough stuff happens to Christians all the time. Death, murder, divorce, thievery, injustice…the list goes on. If we didn't know better, we could fall into a dismal pit of discouragement.

Yet, we know that God loves us even if we don't quite understand what is going on around us. This love is completely encompassing and unconditional. He will never take His love away and no situation, person, or heavenly being can ever change it. His love was so great that He sent His only Son to die for us, while we were yet in our sin. Wrapping our hearts and minds to accept His love helps us to not give up.

We also know that God uses every situation in our lives for good, even the tough times. Nothing escapes His view because He sees every single act of injustice against us. We know that those who live godly lives will suffer persecution. Even though we don't like it, we are comforted by God's hand that directs everything towards our good. He isn't mocked by evil people. They will reap a harvest of judgment for their sins against His sons and daughters.

There's no "oops!" with our Father in heaven. He knows the beginning and the end of our lives as well as those around us. There's no accidents with God—just opportunities to show His glory and grace through those who follow Him with all of their hearts. Take joy, even when many trials come your way, there is a plan, a purpose, and reward for you.

Prayer:

Dear Lord, so many times I get distressed by the trials and unfairness of this life. Yet, I turn to You for hope and strength to get where I need to be in your plan for my life. Amen.

Faith Action:

Every time you start to think that your situation is fate...recite Luke 12:7. Remember that God is in control, and His grace will sustain you.

Day 13: Keep in Step with the Spirit

If we live by the Spirit, let us also keep in step with the
Spirit.
Galatians 5:25

What does it mean to walk with God? Is it really
possible that the God who created this fantastic
universe with all its glory wants to walk with us?
When a baby takes his or her first steps, it's a major
milestone for their physical growth. The same is with
us. When we begin to walk with God, it's the
beginning of our spiritual growth.

Walking with God is different from sprinting (too far
ahead of the Spirit) or standing (too far behind the
Spirit). Walking denotes a rhythmic pace of keeping in
step with the Spirit of God. We sometimes forget how
to walk with God. We stumble through life with
busyness, distractions, annoyances, frustrations, or get
so engaged in our sinful nature that we rarely even
think about walking in the Spirit.

In order to walk physically, there has to be stimulation
from the mind to activate the muscles, bones, and
nerves in the legs. Walking with God begins the same
way, with a change of our mind. Our thinking engages
our walk with God. Are we spiritually paralyzed? It
may be time to deal with our thinking.

When our mind is focused on the sinful nature (or flesh), it will always lead to death, perhaps not physical death right away. But it will certainly lead to death of our dreams, in our relationships and in our destiny.

On the other hand, when our mind is focused on the Spirit, it will always lead to life. We will have renewed hope for our future, we will be forgiven and set free from guilt, and we will have perfect peace even when chaos reigns all around us. We need to have the mind of Christ in order to walk in the Spirit.

Prayer:

Dear Lord, I need the mind of Christ so that I can walk in the Spirit. I pray for your grace and mercy to give me the strength to live as a believer in all areas of my life. Amen.

Faith Action:

Take a walk today and reflect on how you can walk in the Spirit as a witness to those around you.

Day 14: Let Go and Let God

Put out into the deep and let down your nets for a
catch.
Luke 5:4

Peter let down his net into the deep water at Jesus'
instruction even though they fished all night without a
catch. He trusted Jesus at His word despite his own
understanding as a fisherman. As a result, there were
more fish than they could carry and Peter gave his
heart to Jesus. Peter let go of his own knowledge and
experience to let God have His way.

Many times we struggle with letting go and letting
God. We hold on to people and things until there's
hardly anything left. We do this because it's difficult
to let go of relationships, a lifestyle, or things we enjoy
especially if we desire better days and higher hopes.

We want to keep doing what is comfortable and
predictable. Yet, that doesn't always happen the way
we want and God doesn't promise us comfortable
lives. If we choose to let go and let God as Peter did,
there's a risk. God may shake things up so much that
we don't even recognize what we originally had in our
hands.

This is exactly what must happen in order for us to experience a greater relationship with God. We learn to let go of the things that matter of this world and cling to the cross of Jesus Christ. Our affections for people and things will take a second place behind our desires for the Lord.

Sometimes when we let go, God brings those things back to us. Yet, sometimes when we let go, that's the end of it. Either way the Lord is glorified when we let go and learn to trust in Him with all of our hearts. We aren't to be afraid to let go and let God because we will experience a deeper confidence in Christ.

Prayer:

Dear Lord, I struggle with letting this thing in my life go. I need your strength and courage to let go and let You be the Lord of my life in every way. Amen.

Faith Action:

What are you holding on to? Let it go in your mind as you pray. God will take care of it.

Day 15: Sowing and Reaping take Time

See how the farmer waits for the precious fruit of the
earth.
James 5:7

Many times when we've experienced an awakening
from God, we are ready to go right away. However, it
may be awhile before what we believe will come to
pass. We may get excited and jump ahead of what God
wants to do. Some of us jump too quickly to repair a
broken relationship. We may pay tithes/offerings and
expect financial breakthroughs right away. We may
have calling a from God to reach the world for the
gospel, yet it seems like we can't even get past our
own homes.

A farmer who plants a seed doesn't go out the next
day and expect to see a crop. He realizes that it takes
time for the seed to grow root and press through the
ground. It's the same for our spiritual walk in the
Lord, it may be awhile before we see the fruit of our
labor. We can get impatient and want to walk away
from God's calling, many times assuming that perhaps
we missed God somewhere along the way.

We wait patiently on the Lord, for He is good and His
mercy endures forever. God is above and outside of
our time, so He doesn't feel the same urgencies that

we do. Yet, He is faithful to keep His promises, if we would just put our trust in Him, in spite of the odds stacked against us.

There is great joy and calmness that fills our hearts when we accept God's timing over our timing. He's never in a hurry, because He knows the beginning to the ending. Our faith in God is demonstrated when we believe in Him without even seeing the fruit of the work right away. He loves us unconditionally and deeply to do the good work at just the right time.

Prayer:

Dear Lord, help me to wait patiently on You. Sometimes it's tough and I need your assurance that You are in control and I'm not. Help me to trust in the measure of faith You have given me. Amen.

Faith Action:

Plant your favorite herb seed in a pot. Care for it and learn to understand the patience of sowing and reaping.

Day 16: Take the Medicine of Joy

A joyful heart is good medicine.
Proverbs 17:22

Have you ever tried to ride out a headache that wouldn't go away? You finally take medicine and you realize that the headache has lifted. As a result, you can engage with people better, focus more clearly on the job on hand, and have a better attitude all around. This is what happens to believers when they take the medicine of joy to their homes, work, school, and community.

The medicine of joy won't cure every problem that is wrong with our lives. However, it has the power to change the course of any situation that happens along our day. For some of our problems, we have to laugh to keep from crying; yet, even in this, there is redemption from a sluggish attitude.

Unlike our physical medications, which can only be taken at certain times of day and in limited amounts, our joy in the Lord can be renewed every single day. The joy in our hearts isn't limited to the boundaries of everything going just the way we want it all the time. In fact, we could be surrounded by despair, and joy will still throb in our hearts.

Even in tough times, our joy can be ignited when we focus on God's love and plan for our lives. This joy is renewed when we meditate on the grace of God to accept us into the kingdom of Christ. Our joy is full when we remember that we are completely forgiven of our sins, and accepted into the kingdom of God without restraints.

The joy of the Lord can sustain us through trials and temptations. (James 1:2) This doesn't mean we are joyful about our difficulties; rather our joy is because God is control and will help us grow closer to Him through hardship.

Prayer:

Dear Lord, help me to remember to take the medicine of joy when I'm tempted to give into thoughts of despair and anger. Amen.

Faith Action:

Begin to focus on what God has done for you today to help get your joy moving forward.

Day 17: Badge Access

Truly, truly, I say to you, I am the door of the sheep.
John 10:7

Many of us work at jobs where employees can only enter with badge access. Any visitors or vendors have to go through security in order to come in the building. It's tough when you've lost or forgotten your badge, because you will have to go through the same trouble as outsiders. However with your badge, you are welcomed to enter as much as you would like.

When we accepted Jesus Christ as our Lord and Savior, we are granted an incredible badge access. Because of Jesus we can enter into the heavenly gates after we take our last breath here on earth. No one is going to stop us at the door and question our clearance, because we've been washed in the blood of Jesus Christ.

We have badge access to heaven after we die, we have badge access when life gets tough. We are given grace from God to survive and overcome many disruptions to our lives. His grace gives us the strength to move forward, even when we feel weakened in our resolve to complete His calling on our lives.

As believers we also have badge access in our prayer lives. We don't have to offer up sacrifices or do anything out of the ordinary, except have a conversation with our God. Our prayers are immediately heard in the heavenly realms, because God hears His children. The Lord hears and answers our prayers, because He is faithful and desires to move on our behalf.

Just like work, our badge access is only good for us. Our spouses, children, and friends can't use our badge to get into heaven. God doesn't have grandchildren. We each need our own badges in order to enter into His kingdom.

Prayer:

Dear Lord, thank for the badge access to heaven and all the other blessing that You have given me. Strengthen my courage to let others know about this incredible opportunity to know You. Amen.

Faith Action:

Do you have badge access to God? How do you know? Read Romans 10:9-10 to understand how to be saved from your sins.

Day 18: Satan doesn't get to Win

The devil who had deceived them was thrown into the lake of fire and sulfur.
Revelation 20:10

Have you ever had a really tough week where things change quickly both professionally and personally? In those times it seems like everything goes from bad to worse, and we began to feel like our lives are out of control. It can feel like Satan is gaining ground, and we are helplessly watching without any ability to slow his pace. Yet, the truth is that the devil doesn't get to win.

Satan knows that he is in a losing battle, so it's his agenda to take as many people as he can with him. He will do everything it takes to get us to fail. He uses people to frustrate, persecute, and ridicule us. Even if Satan wins a scuffle every now and then, he's losing ground every day.

We stand in the gap for our family and friends that are deceived by the devil as we intercede and witness to them. Our testimony of God's grace and deliverance over our lives is a powerful weapon against the devil. In addition, as we learn God's word, we fight Satan in the battle of our minds speaking God's word of truth to his lies.

The only way Satan can win is if we give up by not praying, not reading God's word, or allowing our sinful nature to dictate our response to difficulty and disappointments. As soldiers of Jesus Christ, we fight back against the enemy every day and never give up. We are equipped with the power of Jesus' name to drive out demons.

Satan never sleeps and he will never stop deceiving until his final day. We don't have to cower in fear because greater is He who is in us than he who is in the world. He is defeated and he doesn't get to win.

Prayer:

Dear Lord, help me to remember that Satan is defeated and to stand up in the name of Jesus against his tactics. I pray for your Spirit to drive me towards victory every single day. Amen.

Faith Action:

What area of your life is losing ground to Satan? Call out to God in prayer and meditate on Romans 12:21, 1 John 2:13, 14, 4:4 and Revelation 20:10 to use against the enemy.

Day 21: Yes and Amen

For all the promises of God find their Yes in him.
2 Corinthians 1:20

Have you ever had someone break a promise to you? It could've been a spouse breaking their marital covenant, or a boss breaking his or her promise of a promotion. Maybe a parent or sibling promised to help you with something, and they let you down. Regardless of who made the promise or what they promised to do, it's hard to trust someone who breaks their promises.

Yet, the promises that God makes to us are always "yes". The Lord will follow through on His promises, because He never lies to us. His promises are good and faithful from now until eternity. They don't expire when the economy crashes or war is declared. God's promises aren't limited by evil people or leaders. He will still accomplish His promises, regardless of who is in control of the government.

When we receive a promise from God, there is a responsibility on our part. It's the "amen" meaning that we agree with the promises of God. There will be many opportunities for us to doubt God's promises. Yet, we can resist doubt and fear by proclaiming in prayer as we stand in agreement with what God promises in His word.

There's a lot that can happen between yes and amen. We are often questioned for our faith in God when it seems like the promise will fall through. Sometimes we are ridiculed for believing in what we can't see at the moment. However, if we continue to pray about His promises and trust in God to fulfill His promises, our strength will be renewed and we will find our "amen".

The only way to know God's promises is to know His word. The reading and meditating of the scriptures will empower our faith to believe beyond what we see in front of us. When we are tempted to doubt, we speak the word of faith from the Bible and we can't help but say "amen".

Prayer:

Dear Lord, I know that every promise from You will be fulfilled in the right time of your perfect will. Grant me the grace to say "amen" in faith to every promise. Amen.

Faith Action:

What is the promise of God that you cling to the most? Look for one of God's many promises in the book of Psalms.

Day 22: Focus on the Promise not the Problem

No unbelief made him waver concerning the promise
of God.
Romans 4:20

Abraham was 75 years old when God made the
promise that he would be the father of a multitude of
nations. For twenty-five years, he continued to believe
in the promise of God, even though his physical body
was withering away every single day.

How did Abraham continue to believe God, when he
knew how old he felt? Abraham didn't waver in the
promise of God, because he kept his focus on the
promise and not the problem. It is problematic for an
elderly couple to have a baby, except for the promise
of God.

Just like Abraham, we have the choice to focus on the
promises of God, or to focus on the problems of our
lives. Abraham didn't deny his problem, he just didn't
focus on it. And we also shouldn't deny that there are
problems in our lives, but we continue to point the
way to the cross. We continue to press forward in our
faith knowing that God will keep His promises to us.

Our problems will be with us until the day of our
death. This sinful world will never run out of

problems. Yet, even problems will have an end, but the promises of God will continue throughout eternity. As believers in the Lord Jesus Christ, we know that the promise of eternal life will happen even before we die. We have the indwelling power and presence of the Holy Spirit to stir up joy in our hearts at the promise of one day being with Jesus.

Focusing on the promise and not the problem is a discipline of our minds. We will be tempted to focus on the problems and all the ways that things can go wrong. Yet, focusing on the problem will tear down our faith and cause us to doubt God's power. When we refuse to waver in God's promises, we will experience the joy of knowing that He keeps His promises.

Prayer:

Dear Lord, I've been focusing on my problems more than focusing on your promises. Grant me the grace to know your promises and walk in faith. Amen.

Faith Action:

Whatever problem you have today, take it to the cross and leave it there. Find a promise of God to build your faith on.

Day 23: I'll be glad when...

But godliness with contentment is great gain.
1 Timothy 6:6

I grew up always saying to myself "I'll be glad when..." I'll be glad when this test is over. I'll be glad when I get to leave the house. I'll be glad when I graduate from school. I'll be glad when this interview is over. I'll be glad when I get a promotion.

We all have the moments of testing and trials when we are looking forward to the ending of one thing so we can move on to another. The problem is that we don't get too much further in the new things, before we are looking forward to its ending as well. Yet, every moment in every season of our lives is used by God. He doesn't waste our joys or sorrows, and everything is leading us towards putting our complete trust in Him.

God is calling us to find contentment in our lives, rather than always desiring the next best thing. Many people on their deathbed regret all the times they rushed through life without really learning to enjoy what was right in front of them. We need to learn to stop and smell the roses in the present moment, because we don't always get another chance.

"I'll be glad when…" is loaded with conditions for our happiness and peace. Yet to be godly and content means that our lives are full, even though we aren't the wealthiest people on earth. We can find our joy in the midst of trials. We can find our purpose in the midst of a jumbled life of activity. We can find a way to enjoy the precious moments of life that are a gift from God to us.

"I'll be glad when…" reveals our lack of faith in God's perfect timing for our lives. He is the master Orchestrator of every believer. The Lord directs our paths to Him, so that we can learn contentment in every situation.

Prayer:

Dear Lord, teach me to be still and learn contentment in my life. I pray for your guidance to lead me in the right ways of truth. Amen.

Faith Action:

Are you tempted to always look forward instead of relaxing in the moment? If you catch yourself feeling discontented, take a moment to thank God for all of His blessings right where you are in life.

Day 24: Just my Portion Please

Give me neither poverty nor riches.
Proverbs 30:8

There are a lot of sad reality TV shows, but one of the most grievous are those which focus on the hoarding of material things. People who live in such bondage have an extremely difficult time letting go and disciplining themselves to live simply. Yet, many of us also have too many things that we never will use. We keep gathering more and more stuff to fill the need that only God can fill in our hearts.

In Proverbs 30, the wise man asked God to give him neither poverty nor riches. He didn't want to be so poor that he would steal and malign the name of God. Neither did he want to be so rich that he would forget that God is his Provider. He wanted his portion that which God has ordained.

What would it be like if Christians asked God to give them only their portion, nothing more, nothing less? We would shop differently, right? We wouldn't need a closet full of clothes, jewelry, and shoes that we can't possibly wear in this lifetime.

Our portion doesn't necessarily mean that we would live in want, but rather we would learn to be content with what we had, rather than always desiring the latest, greatest fashions or homes. Learning to be satisfied with our portion wouldn't just affect our finances, but it would spill over to how we control what we eat or what we say to others.

The Lord promises to provide everything we need according to His riches and glory. However, He didn't promise to give us everything that we want. Many of us have what we need and more (above our portion). Perhaps the Lord allows us to have more than our portion as an opportunity for us to share the good things we have with others who are in need.

Prayer:

Dear Lord, help me to be content with the portion that You have ordained for me. Help me to see when I'm being self-centered and not focused on giving to those in need. Amen.

Faith Action:

What things could you get rid of to live a more simple and contented life? Do you have the courage to do it?

Day 25: His Resources not Mine

And my God will supply every need of yours
according to his riches in glory in Christ Jesus.
Philippians 4:19

Have you ever felt led to give even when you weren't
sure you had enough for yourself? It's one thing for us
to give out of our excess and it's another to give out of
our need. When we have excess of resources, we give
and not really feel any impact from it. However, when
we give out of limited resources, the impact can be felt
much deeper.

What matters most is that we give out of a grateful
heart. We are instructed to give as we have decided in
our hearts, not being reluctant nor under compulsion.
(2 Corinthians 9:7-9) As believers, our giving is
punctuated by joy and not giving to get more from
God. We can't use our gifts as an opportunity to feel
better about ourselves. It's wise for us to take time to
pray and reflect on the reasons we feel led to give.

When we give of our resources cheerfully, we
experience the grace of God in our lives and in the
lives of others. His grace can multiply the smallest of
gifts to do the greatest work for the kingdom of God.
When we give out of what we have, the Lord

replenishes our needs in abundance based on His resources.

God promises to meet every one of our needs according to His riches and glory and not our bank account, 401K, or savings. His blessings go beyond mere earthly treasures towards the presence and power of the Spirit in our lives. We can resist giving in fear or compulsion, and trust in God to lead us in the right direction, even if we don't have all the answers. We will be blessed beyond measure.

Prayer:

Dear Lord, help me to know and hear your voice when it comes to responding to the conviction of giving. Remove any doubt, fear, or selfish motivations from my heart. Fill me with your peace as I continue to trust in You to meet my every need when I need it. Amen.

Faith Action:

Pray and ask God to put a certain amount of offering to give in church before you arrive. Trust in Him to supply of all your needs.

Section 4: Go for Broke

And Elijah said, "As the Lord of hosts lives, before whom I stand, I will surely show myself to him today."

1 Kings 18:15

Background Scripture: 1 Kings 18:1-19

Section 4: Go for Broke!

See, we have left everything and followed you.
Mark 10:28

Obadiah took a great risk hiding 100 prophets of God in caves to spare their lives from Jezebel and at the same time, living in close proximity to King Ahab. He was put on the spot when Elijah instructed him to arrange a meeting with King Ahab.

Obadiah was reluctant because he feared Elijah would change his mind and suddenly disappear. In addition, Elijah was in hiding during the three long years of the famine and King Ahab went to great trouble looking for him, even in other kingdoms. He would only accept by oath that they haven't seen Elijah. Obadiah also didn't want to appear that he knew where Elijah was all along either.

Yet, Elijah was determined to see Ahab whether Obadiah helped him or not. Therefore, Obadiah passed on the message. King Ahab immediately accused Elijah of being a troublemaker; although, he was the one who sold himself out to Jezebel and led the nation to worshipping idols. Elijah was unafraid of King Ahab and gave the order for the king to summon the people as well as the 850 prophets of Baal for a showdown.

Elijah had nothing to lose and everything to gain by following God's command to show himself to Ahab. Soon rain will be released and the famine would end. Since he was called by God for the purpose of revealing His power, Elijah moved forward in faith.

There are many times in our Christian walk when we will have nothing to lose and everything to gain by following God's commands, especially when our lives are all upside down. To go for broke means that we believe all of God's power and ability to get us through it. We hold tightly to His word and loosely to the things of this world. It's all Jesus or nothing at all.

I've been down that road so many times—going for broke spiritually, emotionally, and physically. I pushed myself to do what was right, even though it was painful. It was better for me to lose everything and gain Jesus, than to gain everything and lose my relationship with Him. To hand everything over to God, regardless of the cost, gave me a renewed sense of faith in the living Lord Jesus Christ.

To go for broke in our faith isn't for the fearful nor timid, although there will be times when we step back and take a deep breath. We can't take ground from the devil being anxious and afraid. Our power to overcome isn't from us, but from the Lord. Our faith in God isn't because of what we see, but it is unseen through the assurance of the Holy Spirit.

All things are possible for those who put all of their trust in God and hold nothing back. He reveals Himself to those brave Christians, who step out in faith regardless of the opposition. The next twenty-five devotionals will encourage you to give God everything or get out of the way of those who will.

Day 1: It's all or Nothing

Not one word of all the good promises…had failed; all
came to pass.
Joshua 21:45

When the Israelites set out towards the Promise Land
from Egypt, they were encouraged to move forward by
the promises of God. During the journey, they faced
inward and outward pressure to doubt God and give
into their fears. Many failed to believe and died in the
wilderness because of their unbelief. However, there
were those who continued to hold out and experience
the grace of knowing and seeing God's promises
fulfilled.

Just like the Israelites, we can struggle with doubt and
unbelief in God's promises. We can go through
painful heartbreaks and devastating losses that tempt
us to pull away from the Lord and His word. Yet, if we
press our way through the hurt and disappointment, we
will see the fruition of God's promises in our lives.

God kept every promise to the Israelites even keeping
their clothes and shoes from wearing out after forty
years in the desert. (Deuteronomy 29:5) If God is the
same yesterday, today, and forever more, how much
would He keep His promises to those who serve in the
kingdom faithfully every day?

We aren't perfect in this Christian journey, but we serve a perfect Savior who knows the desires of our hearts. Because we follow Him with a pure heart, the promises of God will be fulfilled in our lives. It's all or nothing…either all the promises of God are yes and amen or none of them are true. (2 Corinthians 1:20)

Our response to the Lord should be the same as our expectations. We determine that it's all or nothing in our journey as we serve, love, and give to the Lord all of our hearts, minds, and souls. We hold back nothing, so that we will see the magnificent joy of the Lord manifested in our lives.

Prayer:

Dear Lord, it's all or nothing for me. I believe in all of your promises to be true and I will serve You every day to give all of my life. Amen.

Faith Action:

What promises of God have you been clinging to? Be unafraid to boldly profess what the Holy Spirit has ignited within you.

Day 2: A Fearless Mother

The Lord is my light and my salvation, whom shall I
fear?
Psalm 27:1

It doesn't matter if you have one or five children, fear
will attempt to grip your heart at one time or another. I
remember how I lovingly took care of my firstborn
son as best I could. However with me standing right
next to him, he stumbled and hit his head on the edge
of the baseboard! At that moment, I realized how
much control I don't have.

Fast forward twenty years, when that same young man
joined the military. As much as I wanted him to
choose a safer start to his adulthood, I knew that I had
to release him into God's hands again. Each of my five
children have shown amazing courage in the face of
fear when they have been tested. I believe that as I
model walking in fearless faith in God, they have
picked it up for themselves.

When a mom trusts in the Lord with all of her heart,
she gives her children the same confidence in God.
They aren't afraid when challenged for their faith.
Fear doesn't grip their hearts when God calls them to
the mission field. It's not presumptuous or foolish risk

taking; rather it's a strong confidence that God will deliver and keep His promises according to His word.

The Lord is the mother's light and salvation; therefore she has nothing to fear for her children. She knows that God will keep and direct them along the way. Fear will test a mother's heart and mind, especially at night. However she reminds herself that God hasn't given her a spirit of fear, but of power, love, and of sound mind so she sleeps in peace.

Prayer:

Dear Lord, I pray that You will continually strengthen my heart to trust in You and that fear will find no place here. Let me be the example of a fearless mother so that my children will learn to step out in faith and courage. Amen.

Faith Action:

In your mind, hand each of your children to God for His purpose and plan for their lives.

Day 3: Is Jesus Ignoring me?

But he did not answer her a word.
Matthew 15:23

A Canaanite woman cried out to Jesus to heal her daughter vexed by a demon spirit. Jesus appeared to not pay any attention to her and she still kept after Him. The disciples were weary of her, and asked Jesus to send her away. Jesus replied, "I was sent only to the lost sheep of the house of Israel." She fell on her knees and begged for mercy.

Jesus explained that it wasn't fair to take food from the family (Jews) to feed the puppies (Gentiles). The Canaanite woman didn't miss a beat when she replied that even the puppies eat crumbs from the table. Jesus was amazed at the faith of this Gentile woman. Her daughter was healed in that moment.

The Canaanite woman could've gave up. She could've shrugged her shoulders and walked away thinking she wasn't good enough, not religious enough, or not Jewish at all. She had a certain gumption that wouldn't let go of Jesus, even when He seemed hesitant right in front of her.

It was though He was pulling on her to dig deep in her faith to not let Him go, until He healed her daughter.

While the disciples were regularly exposed to Jesus' miracles, the Canaanite woman was not, and yet she had the faith to believe in Him. Jesus wants us to not give up even when it seems like He may not be listening.

We have to dig deep in our faith and refuse the lies of the enemy in our minds. We cling and pray God's promises from the word, even though everything around us seems to be going in the opposite direction. It's impossible for God to fail His word, He will accomplish everything He promised to do in our lives. Keep praying. Keep trusting. He will move in our behalf.

Prayer:

Dear Lord, I press. I press. I press into You for everything I need to do your good will. I can do nothing without You. Send your deliverance in my life. Amen.

Faith Action:

What are you pressing into Jesus about in prayer? Imagine yourself as the Canaanite woman who cried out to Jesus for mercy. Pray your prayer of faith based on 1 John 5:14-15.

Day 4: What to do when I don't Know What to Do

God of our Lord Jesus Christ may give you the spirit
of wisdom.
Ephesians 1:17

Have you ever had times when you were stumped on
what to do? Perhaps a crisis has hit your family and
you are unsure of what would be the first right step. Or
maybe you find yourself in a quandary in which you
need to make an important decision, and you have no
idea of what to do. It's in these moments that we turn
to God for wisdom and revelation.

Paul prayed for the Ephesians that God would give
them the spirit of wisdom and revelation in the
knowledge of Him. He also asked that their eyes
would be enlightened to know the hope given to them,
the riches of his glorious inheritance in the saints, and
His immeasurable power to those who believe. We can
pray this prayer for ourselves and others when we
don't know what to do.

God reveals to us what to do when we come to Him in
faith about our situation. He gives us the grace to hear
His voice and to trust in His direction. This doesn't
always happen right away as we are constantly
distracted by other things. However, when we stop and

give God our full attention, He blesses us with the wisdom and revelation on the next steps.

As we consistently turn to Him for direction, we become more able to hear and know the right way to go. We can look back on all the times where God has shown us the right way so that we can trust Him for direction in the new things. It's not that God isn't speaking, it's that we need to turn to Him with more earnest attention for wisdom and revelation.

Prayer:

Dear Lord, I need to hear from You. Show me your wisdom and revelation in what to do. Please enlighten my eyes to understanding the next best steps. Amen.

Faith Action:

Are you at a place where you don't know what to do? Make Ephesians 1:17-23 into a prayer for enlightenment.

Day 5: Uncomfortable in the Calling

Oh, my Lord, I am not eloquent.
Exodus 4:10

When God called Moses to lead the Israelites out of Egypt, there was reluctance. Not on God's part, but on Moses' part. He struggled with the idea that he would be expected to speak to a large group of people on the behalf of God. Yet, after some point in the journey, Moses began to speak to the people.

When God calls us to do His good work, we may not always be comfortable in the calling. Sometimes we can be like Moses—coming up with all the excuses of why we aren't the ones to do His will in a certain manner.

However, feeling uncomfortable is normal and probably good for the majority of believers. As long as we believe that we can do the calling of God in our own strength, we are bound to fail miserably. Yet, when we trust in God to provide us everything we need for His great work, we show the glory of God.

The Lord is glorified when great things are done through us. This happens when we recognize that the great ability within us isn't because we are so gifted and talented. But rather, that God has chosen us as the vessels of His grace and strength. God takes our small contribution of the calling, and He brings greater blessing with people giving their lives to Christ or experiencing a significant deliverance from the enemy.

Prayer:

Dear Lord, please increase my strength to follow everything that You have called me to do. Help me to trust in You, even though I may be uncomfortable in the calling. Amen.

Faith Action:

Are you uncomfortable in your calling? Find your peace by meditating on Philippians 1:6 every day and night.

Day 6: Risk of Faith

Now faith is the assurance of things hoped for, the
conviction of things not seen.
Hebrews 11:1

Abraham was led from the comfort of everything and
everyone he knew—to go to an unknown land with a
promise that wouldn't be fulfilled for many years.
Abraham took the risk of faith, in spite of not being
able to fully understand. We can imagine his difficult
conversation with Sarah and her following him
without a complete understanding of the situation. It
must have been hard on her to wrap her mind around
what they were doing. What made them take such a
great risk of faith? It was the faith he had in God.

How many of us are willing to take the risk of faith?
Many times what is a risk of faith can look terribly
ridiculous or foolish. Take those who've sold
everything they own and moved to another country in
order to share the gospel with the lost. Take someone
who shares the gospel with a hurting co-worker at the
risk of being reprimanded by their boss. What is
foolishness to those in the world, could be the risk of
faith that God is expecting from His children.

A risk of faith in the Lord isn't some presumptuous or
foolish act. It's a deliberate, prayerful trust in God,

regardless of the circumstances. This step of faith is just the beginning of a relationship with God. Those who continue to grow in Jesus Christ will find the risks becoming greater with each step. Faith is meant to grow every day, being seen in action and not just words.

It's not so difficult to take the risk of faith when we are focused more on who God is and less on our abilities. What is certainly impossible with man, is very much possible with God. There is nothing He won't do for those who put their trust in Him.

Prayer:

Dear Lord, You are the one that I put my trust in, and I'm willing to take the risk of faith that will result in your glory. Give me the strength and courage to trust in You. Amen.

Faith Action:

What is the risk of faith that God is calling on your life? What is keeping you from taking that risk?

Day 7: Where is your Faith?

*Each according to the measure of faith that God has
assigned.*
Romans 12:3

A friend quit her well-paying job to stay at home to
raise her children. A godly couple with two young
daughters sold all their possessions to move to a third
world country while they were still learning to speak
the language. A young woman quits college to pursue
the mission field. What makes people step out of their
comfort zone to the realm of the unknown? It is faith.

Each believer is given a measure of faith by God to do
what He has called them. This measure of faith can be
stretched way beyond what we think it should be for
us. However, there's no greater satisfaction than
knowing that God is in control and moving out in faith
because of it.

People who've found their faith and followed the
leading of the Holy Spirit are often cautioned and
sometimes ridiculed. Sadly, many of those doubters
come from the body of Christ. And most likely from
those who lost their faith and need to recover it.

Rediscovering one's faith in God is risky…*will He
call me to a hard place?* Maybe or maybe not. It's not

hard when the vision has already taken hold of our soul. We wake up to it. It drives us throughout our day and visits us in our dreams at night. What might seem to others as foolishness for us is the call and determination of God on our lives. We can't find any other place for satisfaction and peace.

Where is your faith? Did you lose it when you found the dream job? Did you lose it when you got married and had children? The wonderful thing about serving our God is that it's never too late to find our faith. It may have a different look and feel than when we first saw it, but it will manifest itself in the perfect way as we surrender to the Lord.

Prayer:

Dear Lord, I need to rediscover my faith in You for this life journey. Strengthen my heart with courage and peace as I follow your word in faith. Amen.

Faith Action:

Have you lost your faith? Ask the Lord to awaken you back on the right path by praying and meditating on Luke 1:37.

Day 8: Emotional Disengagement

Do not take to heart all the things that people say.
Ecclesiastes 7:21

Many people have emotionally disengaged themselves in a negative manner. Perhaps they've been hurt by others, so they throw up a wall to keep people out. This isn't healthy nor helpful in many relationships. However, there is a place for a healthy emotional disengagement, especially when you are in conflict with a family member, friend, or co-worker.

This emotional disengagement is about taking your emotions/feelings about the issue and setting them temporarily aside. Many times we get upset and angry about a situation to the point where we are unable to resolve the problem. Our emotions are easily manipulated by the desires of our sinful nature, which only seeks our pleasure instead of humbling ourselves.

When we step back and emotionally disengage, we allow a spiritual engagement to take its course. Spiritual engagement means that we ask ourselves the question "what would God have me do?" We place ourselves out of the emotional upheaval and begin to see the situation from an eternal perspective.

We ask questions such as: will this situation matter when I stand before God one day? Have I handled it in a way that God will say to me "Well done!" Or will I suffer loss because of my pride and selfishness? We must also take into account the spiritual maturity of the other person and ask ourselves the question: will my response give this person a true reflection of Christ in me?

Emotional disengagement and spiritual engagement doesn't mean that we just roll over and let the other person step all over us and the issue. Rather, it's a calculated and thoughtful response that reflects spiritual maturity and a Christ-like attitude. When we choose Christ, we are given wisdom above our human abilities to respond in the best manner.

Prayer:

Dear Lord, help me to know when I'm becoming more emotionally than spiritually engaged in a conflict. Give me the strength to tone down my emotions and respond in the most loving spiritual engagement. Amen.

Faith Action:

Spiritually engage yourself to hear and obey God's calling on your life even if you need to emotionally disengage from specific people.

Day 9: Fear isn't from God

For God gave us a spirit not of fear but of power and
love and self-control.
2 Timothy 1:7

It's hard to read the news and not get afraid for
yourself, your family, and friends. The random
violence across the world is shocking and deplorable.
It seems like people have completely turned away
from God or even the idea that they will have to give
an account for their atrocious sins against humanity.

Yet, even in this dire state of sinfulness, there is an
answer: Jesus Christ. Knowing Jesus as Lord of our
lives gives us peace in the midst of great wickedness.
We don't have to live in a state of fear. We are called
by God to courageously live our lives out in power,
love, and self-control.

The Holy Spirit fills our heart with hope and strength
to move forward, even when our knees are shaky and
palms are sweaty. We can trust in the Lord to protect
us in times of trouble and He will never leave us when
it gets difficult. His presence will calm our anxious
hearts, and His word will engage our minds to focus
on truth instead of lies.

When we find ourselves afraid, we must step back and reflect on who God is. Do we believe that God is in control at all times? Do we trust that He can make all things work together for our good? Do we believe in the power of His word?

Fear is a spirit that can be dealt with by God's word. We can speak to ourselves quietly or shout out loud that God hasn't given us a spirit of fear, but of love, power, and self-control. We can also remind ourselves that perfect love drives out all fear. (1 John 4:18) Our God is more than able to keep us until the day He calls us home to heaven. We are invincible in Christ!

Prayer:

Dear Lord, I don't want fear to reign over my life. Regardless of my life situation, help me to trust in your powerful hand to lead me in the right place and protect me along the way. Amen.

Faith Action:

Replace fear in your life with courage from God's word. Memorize 2 Timothy 1:7 and repeat it to yourself every day.

Day 10: What's on your Mind?

We have the mind of Christ.
1 Corinthians 2:16

After many years of playing tennis and watching my children in their sports activities, I've realized that athleticism and talent is secondary to mental focus. If I can't focus my mind to drown out all the other voices, I will lose. In sports, they call it the zone. It's when a player is so focused on the game they don't hear the roar of the crowd or any other distractions. If we want to walk in the Spirit, we need to get in the spiritual zone.

Our mind brings us into the zone. When we are spiritually connected to God, we're not distracted by the flurry of activity around us. We learn to trust the Holy Spirit within to guide, direct, and lead us into the right paths.

We can have the mind of Christ when we meditate on the Word of God. (Psalm 119:15) Meditation is simply rehearsing what God's word says over and over in our minds. As a result, we aren't nudged so easily by our carnal nature to do those things which are sinful.

We can also invite the Holy Spirit's guidance. (John 16:13) The Holy Spirit gives direction and guidance in our Christian walk. It's so easy for us to dismiss the urgings of the Spirit, when our minds are so busy with everything else.

We can nurture our minds with Bible study. (2 Timothy 2:15) Being involved in a Bible study challenges our faith and helps us to become more knowledgeable. Every answer necessary for our lives is in the Bible.

We can also discipline our minds. (2 Corinthians 10:5) We discipline our minds like our bodies by filtering what we allow into it. By cutting off unhealthy visual and auditory prompts, we can restrain our thoughts.

Spiritual growth over sinful desires is possible. It comes day-by-day, step-by-step with a determined spirit, an open heart, and changed mind. Aren't you tired of losing to your sinful nature?

Prayer:

Dear Lord, help me have the mind of Christ in all things. Give me the strength to discipline myself to grow up spiritually. Amen.

Faith Action:

Begin to train your mind like you would an exercise plan for your body. Keep directing it to God's word for every situation in your life.

Day 11: Is Jesus Enough?

My soul will be satisfied as with fat and rich food.
Psalm 63:5

Most of us would answer the question "Is Jesus enough?" with a resounding yes! However, if we carefully examined our relationship with Him, we might say Jesus is enough in addition to a spouse, a new job, car, house, etc.

Is Jesus enough? If He never answered another prayer, is He still enough? If the only thing we receive from Jesus is a trip to heaven, would He be enough? Jesus gives us more than enough based on His word in Ephesians 3:20 "Now to him who is able to do far more abundantly than all that we ask or think, according to the power at work within us."

It's a good daily practice to reflect and focus on our relationship with Jesus. If we start our mornings with a simple prayer of "Jesus, I want You to be enough in my life today", we would find ourselves more satisfied with the outcomes of our day. This is because we learn to have a Jesus focus instead of a 'me-focus'.

Jesus is more than enough even if everything else is falling apart. He comes when we need Him most to comfort, lead, and empower us through the Holy Spirit

Adversity is a part of our Christ walk when we reflect on what Jesus said in Luke 12:51-52 "Do you think that I have come to give peace on earth? No, I tell you, but rather division. For from now on in one house there will be five divided, three against two and two against three."

We resist adversity because we enjoy keeping ourselves from the messiness of it. However, with the help of the Holy Spirit, we can pray and seek God's wisdom in dealing with adversity so that He can work the greater good in our lives as well as in those who are around us.

Prayer:

Dear Lord, help me push past adversity and towards your will for my life. Give me the strength and courage to deal with it instead of always trying to ignore it. Amen.

Faith Action:

What adversity do you need to push past today? Receive your strength from the Holy Spirit to push past it.

Day 14: Stretch Assignments

Each according to the measure of faith that God has
assigned.
Romans 12:3

Oftentimes in the business world, employees who
want to move up in the company are given stretch
assignments. These assignments aren't set up for their
failure, but rather to help them expand their talents,
gifts, and mental abilities to accomplish a project.
Many times employees don't know what they can do,
until they are in a position where they need to figure
things out for themselves.

God often gives His people stretch assignments as
well. He allows us to deal with trials and situations
that we feel incapable of working out. It's in these
times, that we discover more about God's power
within us that gives us the ability to overcome
insurmountable problems.

If God were to ask our permission for these faith-
stretching assignments, most (if not all) of us would
respond with a resounding "No, thank you." Many
times these tasks are exceptionally difficult, and we
feel like there's no way this situation can ever work
itself out.

However, it's in these tasks that we discover our faith in God, our ability to pray through difficulty, and our deepening understanding of God's word. While we are in the process of the assignment, we are growing up spiritually and it's evident to those around us. Our prayers become more intense and focused. Our everyday choices become more in tune with the application of living God's word and not just hearing it.

Even better, we can believe God for the miraculous and we aren't afraid to share our beliefs with other people. When our stretch assignment has been completed, we will be more ready for the next one, because we know what our God can do even with a tiny mustard seed of faith. (Luke 17:6)

Prayer:

Dear Lord, I feel like I'm in a faith-stretching assignment that is well beyond me. I need your wisdom and insight to finish this task well. Amen.

Faith Action:

Write down your stretch assignment from God. Put it in a place where you can pray it every morning and night.

Day 15: Spiritual Hunger Pains

Blessed are those who hunger and thirst for
righteousness, for they shall be satisfied.
Matthew 5:6

When I was growing up my dad would make large
Sunday dinners for our family. Our stomachs would
growl as we smelled the fried chicken, gravy, mashed
potatoes, and green beans all day. The downside of
those dinners was that dad also enjoyed Sunday
football. This meant that he would regularly stop
cooking to watch a football play. Unfortunately, that
meant that our Sunday dinners were usually later
instead of earlier in the day. No one had to call any of
us twice when dinner was finally ready.

Our physical bodies remind us when we need to eat.
We can fill that need with healthy food, unhealthy
food, or we can ignore it. Most of the time, if we are
able, we will not ignore our stomachs growling, except
in times of fasting. However what are we doing about
our spiritual hunger pains? Are we filling it with
healthy or unhealthy habits? Or are we ignoring it?

Our spiritual hunger pains tend to hit us when we've
been neglecting our times of Bible study, prayer, and
Christian fellowship. We are reminded that we are
spiritually hungry when our lives began to unravel or

headaches or high blood pressure. Knowing the destruction of fear, how can we overcome it?

Fear is overcome by faith in God's word. When we know what God speaks to our situation, we find a peaceful presence takes over our hearts. Fear is overcome by the love of God. When we rest in the unconditional love of God for us and our families, we can release them to fulfill God's purpose for their lives. Fear is overcome by truth. When we know the truth, we are set free from the bondages of living in fear.

Prayer:

Dear Lord, I resist the spirit of fear, because You have given me power, love, and self-control. I pray for your hand over my life every single day to walk in faith, truth, and love. Amen.

Faith Action:

What is God telling you to "Fear not?" Write it down on a sheet of paper, pray for God's strength and peace, then tear it up and throw away in faith.

Day 17: Fight the Good Fight

Fight the good fight of the faith.
1Timothy 6:12

God has directed us to fight (not each other), but to fight in the faith. Our trials, tribulations, and problems are opportunities for our faith to show up, instead of our sinful nature of worry and anxiousness. Fighting and resisting our enemy, Satan, may not come natural for us, but it's a necessary part of our Christian journey.

Fighting the good fight of faith is a call for us to never give up, even when we are struggling just to stay in the war. Many times we feel weakened by the desires of our sinful nature and the disappointments of life that haven't worked out for us. As tempting as it is to throw in the towel and give up, it's important that we push ourselves forward in the faith.

Giving up instead of fighting in the faith doesn't guarantee an end to our struggles. Giving up the faith in the midst of a trial only means that our situation can get worse. Yet, even in the worst part of a spiritual battle, God makes a way for us to escape, if we would turn to Him for renewed strength.

We were never meant to fight by ourselves. The Lord is our constant companion throughout the tough journeys of life, and He sends people our way to help us as well. When we accept that the battle is part of being in the faith, we aren't so thrown off when bad things happen.

It's a good fight in the faith because God has a plan, and He's working it for our good. This fight is worth it, because our loved ones will come to know God as we pray earnestly for them. This fight is a part of what we do as believers.

Prayer:

Dear Lord, I want to fight the good fight of faith. I need your Spirit to empower me with hope, strength, and courage to move forward every day. Amen.

Faith Action:

Professional competitors have to work hard in order to be ready for engagement. What spiritual exercises, could you do in order to be ready for the good fight?

Day 18: Don't Fake it…Face it

We are afflicted in every way, but not crushed.
2 Corinthians 4:8

As believers in Jesus Christ we can feel the pressure to not own up to our own weaknesses or problems. Yet Christians suffer just like unbelievers. Christians have marital problems that sometimes end in separation or divorce. Christians have family members who suffer with physical, emotional, or mental illnesses. Christians have children who turn away from truth and turn towards immorality, drugs, or alcohol. Christians lose their jobs and have trouble finding another one. There's no denying or faking away our problems.

Facing our problems doesn't mean that we shout out our personal business in the streets. Rather, we are transparent and honest about our complete dependency on an invisible God. We live in such a way that reveals the presence of Jesus Christ even in our weaknesses. We face the fact that we live in a fallen world where sin abounds, yet the grace of God abounds even more!

The grace given to believers helps us cope with the problems of our lives. When we turn to God in prayer concerning our weaknesses, He renews hope and strength in our hearts to keep moving forward. We are led and driven by His love that assures us that we aren't alone in our suffering. The Lord supplies ample wisdom for us to know what to do when we are confused or perplexed by our trials.

Facing our problems instead of pretending they don't exist becomes a testimony to those God has placed around us. They see how our affliction doesn't have the last say in our lives, instead they witness the resilient hope of Jesus in our words and actions. Jesus lives and because He lives, we can face tomorrow.

Prayer:

Dear Lord, I've been hit low with problems, and I'm tempted to pretend they don't exist. Help me Lord with your strength to face my issues as a testimony of your presence in my life. Amen.

Faith Action:

How do you deal with your issues? Make a commitment in your heart and mind to courageously face your issues with God's help.

Day 19: Giants or Grasshoppers

We seemed to ourselves like grasshoppers.
Numbers 13:33

The Israelites were finally close to the Promised Land when Moses sent 12 men to spy it out. They've survived the years of slavery, they watched the miraculous plagues on the Egyptians, they witnessed the parting of the Red Sea, and they ate manna. If that wasn't enough, they saw the visible presence of God as a cloud by day and a fire by night.

However, 10 of the 12 spies gave a bad report of the giants in the land and compared themselves to grasshoppers. Instead of focusing on the greatness and power of God, who brought them out of Egypt, they compared themselves to the inhabitants of the land and become discouraged. This spread through the camp like a wildfire on a dry day and many of the Israelites couldn't believe in God's promises. As a result, only Caleb and Joshua would live to see and enjoy the Promised Land.

Before we can judge the Israelites, we must take a good look at ourselves. Many times, the Lord will place what seems to be an impossible idea in our hearts and minds. We are initially excited just like the Israelites, but soon find ourselves incredibly discouraged when we face difficulty in the journey. Instead of seeing how God will come through for us, regardless of the opposition, we see our situation as greater than God. Just because it gets hard, doesn't mean that we are to give up on the calling.

James Hudson Taylor wrote, "There are three stages in the work of God: impossible, difficult, done." God will complete His work in us and we will make it to the Promised Land as long as our eyes remain on Him. However, as long as we are looking at ourselves without God's support, we will see grasshoppers. Everything we need to accomplish His will is doable as we step out in faith and believe in God against all odds.

Prayer:

Dear Lord, help me to keep my eyes on You and not on my limitations. I know that I can accomplish everything You called me to do in Christ's name. Amen.

Faith Action:

What makes you a giant or grasshopper of faith? Begin with sharing your giant-sized dream with those who are also called out of their comfort zone.

Day 20: How bad do you Want It?

Then I proclaimed a fast there.
Ezra 8:21

Ezra had a great journey ahead to lead a large group of Jewish people back to their homeland. He would need protection for defenseless men, women, and children. Ezra shared with King Artaxerxes how the Lord God was good to those who followed Him, and how His great power was against those who forsook Him. After this bold proclamation, Ezra didn't want to ask the king for military protection in their journey back. Instead he fasted and prayed. God heard Ezra's prayer for guidance and protection towards their destination.

There comes a time in every believer's life when we have to ask ourselves the question "how bad do I really want this prayer answered?" If it's an urgent and necessary need, we will make time for fasting and prayer.

Fasting isn't easy for most of us. Our sinful nature demands satisfaction whether it's giving up food, social media, TV, recreation, or anything that brings us pleasure. Yet, fasting is a great way for us to clear out the distractions of our desires, so that we can truly pray and seek God's guidance.

Once we've felt the calling to fast, we can find every excuse to break it or postpone it for another time. This is when we must push ourselves to follow through and seek God's strength to do so. Repeated failure in fasting is a sign that our sinful nature has a greater dominance over our lives.

Fasting isn't meant to prove how spiritual we are, actually true heartfelt fasting is humbling and reveals how much we need God's help. It gives us perspective and insight into our inner spiritual need over the physical needs, so that we can have a greater confidence in our prayers to God.

Prayer:

Dear Lord, many times I've struggled with fasting, yet I want to grow up spiritually with this discipline in my life. I pray for the strength to fast and pray. Amen.

Faith Action:

Think of something you could give up for one month in order to pray for a God intervention.

Day 21: Not Ordinary but Extraordinary

And whatever he did, the LORD made it succeed.
Genesis 39:23

When Joseph's brothers saw him, their jealous eyes could only see an ordinary boy who was the favorite son of their father, yet they eventually bowed down to him. When Potiphar first met Joseph, he saw a common slave, yet he eventually made him an overseer over everything in his house. When the jailer first knew Joseph, he saw an accused prisoner whom he eventually put in charge of all the prisoners. When Pharaoh first saw Joseph, he hoped for a potential seer to help him with a dream, but he eventually made Joseph second in command.

Just like Joseph, we are initially only seen through people's first perception of us. "She's only a single mom." "She's only a wife of that man." "He's only a worker on the line." "He's only a kid." It doesn't matter whatever ordinary titles are placed on us, we are seen by God as extraordinary people with purpose.

Those same people who may put us down, don't know that we are interceding for their souls. They don't know that we are praying for wisdom on our jobs. They don't know that God has a greater purpose for us and that we aren't defined by what we do, but rather by whom we serve.

In 2 Corinthians 4:7, we understand that "we have this treasure in jars of clay, to show that the surpassing power belongs to God and not to us". The power of God within us gives us the ability to accomplish our dreams and destiny beyond what we could do in our natural talent or strengths. He blesses us with everything we need to surpass the ordinary and fly to the extraordinary life that God calls us to achieve.

Prayer:

Dear Lord, help me to resist the ordinary thoughts about myself and give me the grace to rise to the extraordinary plans You have for me. Amen.

Faith Action:

Write down on several index cards the extraordinary calling God has on your life. Place them in strategic places around your home to remind you of God's calling on your life.

Day 22: Praying for the Impossible

And he believed the LORD, and he counted it to him as
righteousness.
Genesis 15:6

Have you ever been exhausted waiting for God to answer your prayers? Or have you ever prayed for something so much bigger than you, that only a God-intervention makes it happen? Sometimes it feels like biting off more than you can chew.

Abraham must have felt that way. He was frustrated because he was promised to have children numbering as the stars in the sky. Yet years later, he was still childless. Eliezer was Abraham's head servant and destined to become the heir of the household. For Eliezer to become Abraham's heir, he wouldn't have to believe God. His feeling was the same as ours when we don't feel like God is going to answer: whatever happens…happens. It's when believing God in prayer becomes too hard.

But God wanted Abraham to press forward in faith. God also wants us to press forward in faith as well, in spite of our weaknesses. We could just throw up our hands and give up. It feels much easier in the short run, but if we do, we will always wonder what would've happened if we pressed in faith and believed God.

Prayers of faith may take time, effort, and patience. Yet, it's the best way because the outcome results in the total glory going to God. For Abraham and Sarah to have a child in their old age was God. There's no other explanation for two elderly people to have a son that would lead to the birth, death, and resurrection of our Lord Jesus Christ. God got the glory!

It's the same with us. God will get the glory when we press forward in prayer and faith. We refuse to give up or give in, and God will honor it with answered prayer.

Prayer:

Dear Lord, increase my faith to have greater trust in You when everything is pushing me towards giving up. I want to trust you more. Amen.

Faith Action:

Find a creative way to express your prayer of faith for the impossible. Use a collage, draw a picture, or anything that would speak to your heart a strong faith.

Day 23: It's *not that* Complicated

Whoever has the Son has life; whoever does not have
the Son of God does not have life.
1 John 5:12

Have you ever heard someone explain a situation
beginning with "It's complicated"? Typically that
means that we can only understand their situation by
hearing everything from beginning to end. People who
generally use this expression don't want you to
understand the situation, because you might find it
more uncomplicated that what they are saying.

Many religions have complicated ways for people to
attain salvation. They may have to work for it by
following rigorous, strict lifestyles. Or they must
constantly free their minds of any convictions about
right or wrong. The truth is that anything that steps
away from the grace of God through Christ Jesus will
eventually hit a complicated moment.

Jesus made it very clear in John 14:6 that no one
comes to the Father except through the Son. There are
no exceptions no matter how good or fair you are. To
reject Jesus Christ's sacrifice for our sins is to
complicate our eternal future.

Knowing Jesus Christ isn't complicated, it's a matter of confessing that we are sinners and believing that He came as a sacrifice for our sins. The inner peace that floods our soul is the assurance that we are free from sin.

Let's not complicate the message of Christ, those who are drawn by the Spirit will respond with brokenness and a readiness to serve God. Every true believer in Jesus Christ will experience that transformation from being in darkness to knowing the light. They will also have the assurance of the Holy Spirit to know God more intimately. The inner peace of God isn't complicated for those who long for eternal life.

Prayer:

Dear Lord, I pray that You will help me clearly share the message of Christ with those who are lost. Amen.

Faith Action:

Write out your personal testimony of going from the darkness of sin to the light of Jesus. When an opportunity comes to share the message of Christ, begin with your testimony.

Day 24: You Snooze...You Lose

A little sleep, a little slumber...and poverty will come
upon you like a robber.
Proverbs 6:10-11

Many people find themselves living in spiritual, emotional, mental, physical, and financial poverty every day. When lack of motivation keeps us from stretching beyond our own limitations, poverty in every level becomes one of the greatest travesties of life.

Many of us are snoozing our way through life, without purpose or direction, even though God has a plan for every single person. We live in a world where we can daydream and discuss our desires for decades, without actually accomplishing anything. Our inability to press through this mindset of poverty can numb us to the point of merely existing, rather than thriving from one stretch of faith to the next.

How do we keep from snoozing so that we don't lose God's purpose for our lives? We first recognize that God has a job for us to do in this lifetime. Since we don't know the exact moment of our death, we take every day as a gift from God to accomplish His will. We don't sleep walk to work from morning to evening while drifting towards Friday. Instead, we show up ready, willing, and seeking what God-interventions are happening that day.

Secondly, we refuse to settle for second-best in our daily choices. We will always be tempted to settle for the easy tasks that don't require faith-stretching opportunities. Instead we look for the impossibilities and believe in God's purpose to reveal His glory in a majestic way.

A Christian snoozer is going to be a loser in the end. We will all give an account of what we did with what God has given us. Get up and get busy because life is too short to miss the day of your visitation!

Prayer:

Dear Lord, I recognize my sin of not stretching my faith beyond the predictable. I pray for your strength to press forward and awake to living life to the fullest. Amen.

Faith Action:

What are you procrastinating on that God is leading you to complete? Every day do something (regardless of how small it seems) that moves you closer to achieving your goals.

Day 25: Never Give Up Hope

And let us not grow weary of doing good, for in due
season we will reap, if we do not give up.
Galatians 6:9

My daughter was playing in a difficult volleyball game
and they were losing pretty badly to a stronger team. I
reminded her to play her best because she's not
supposed to hand the game over because the other
team looks intimidating. She may lose the game, but
they will have to work for it.

Sometimes this Christian walk is tough and we may
want to throw in the towel. We are tempted on every
side to live for ourselves, instead of living for God.
We are pressed into prayer and Bible study to stay
close to God. We are burdened with the cares of our
family and friends. We sometimes get tired of waiting
on God.

Yet we can never give up on God. We may fail in our
efforts, but God never fails. Many impossibilities
stand in our way, but nothing is impossible with God.
We feel overwhelmed and broken, but God is with us
and strengthens according to His power. We can't
always understand what is going on, yet God knows
the beginning to the end.

Because we are His children, we have hope and hope doesn't disappoint us. (Romans 5:5) Many situations will disappoint us and people will let us down; however, the deep urgings in our souls come from the Holy Spirit. He encourages and prepares us for the next step in our journey. We can't give up just because it gets hard. We are spiritually gifted to see our situation beyond what we see in our natural eyes. There's great peace and victory for us on the other side, if we just keep pressing forward in faith. We are destined for overcoming the most difficult challenges, because of God's hand on our lives.

Prayer:

Dear Lord, I'm tempted to give up every single day. Yet, I turn to You for renewed strength and vision to accomplish your great will. I pray for your presence to go with me along the way. Amen.

Faith Action:

Find a promise of God and write it on a ball that you can toss up to remind yourself when your faith is tested.

About the author

Crystal McDowell is a writer, speaker, and teacher with a passion to encourage believers to grow in their relationship with Jesus Christ through practical application of God's word. As a freelance writer, editor, and blogger for over 15 years, Crystal has published numerous Christian curriculums as well as many articles. She writes daily devotionals for women at daughtersofthecreator.com. One day when she grows up, above all, she hopes to hear from her Creator and Father..."Well done, thou good and faithful daughter."

SERIOUSLY GOD?

Volume 2

Continue to follow the life of Elijah from his challenge
to the pagan prophets to his wondrous exit by a fiery
chariot with four sections including:

Glory belongs to God
Give yourself Time
Get Back to Work
Great Days Ahead

AVAILABLE SEPTEMBER 2016

36339727R00129

Made in the USA
San Bernardino, CA
20 May 2019